great soup
empty bowls

great soup
empty bowls

recipes from the Empty Bowls Fundraiser

executive editor Jamie Kennedy | photographer Christopher Freeland

whitecap

Edited by Alison Maclean
Technical edit by Glenys Morgan
Proofread by Lesley Cameron
Cover and interior design by Roberta Batchelor
Cover and interior photographs by Christopher Freeland
Food styling by Carol Dudar
Prop styling by Marc-Philippe Gagne, Oksana Slavutych

Special thanks to Ace Bakery for donating bread for the food photography.
The following people donated their time to this fundraising project:
Carol Dudar, Christopher Freeland, Marc-Philippe Gagne, Susan Jefferies,
Jamie Kennedy, Alison Maclean, Oksana Slavutych.

PRINTED AND BOUND IN CANADA

National Library of Canada Cataloguing in Publication Data
Great soup, Empty Bowls

Includes index.
ISBN 1-55285-347-0

1. Soups. I. Kennedy, Jamie.
TX757.G73 2002   641.8'13   C2002-910195-6

The publisher acknowledges the support of the Canada Council for the Arts
and the Cultural Services Branch of the Government of British Columbia for our
publishing program. We acknowledge the financial support of the Government
of Canada through the Book Publishing Industry Development Program for our
publishing activities.

ROYALTIES FROM THIS BOOK WILL GO TO THE ANISHNAWBE STREET PATROL

The Gardiner Museum
of Ceramic Art

Introduction

In 1992, Sue Jefferies, Assistant Curator of Ceramics at the Gardiner Museum telephoned me to talk about a fundraising event she wanted to stage at the museum. It was called Empty Bowls and it would benefit the Anishnawbe Street Patrol. The fundraiser would bring together the talents of cooks and potters in the form of an affordable charity to benefit those in need of food and shelter. The idea caught my attention right away. It seemed manageable and I liked the feel of it.

Professional cooks are often asked to participate in fundraisers. I always want to participate, but sometimes I do have to say no. Too often our efforts get lost in the layers of organization required to choreograph such undertakings and we end up far from the spirit of the project. That is not the case with Empty Bowls. Quite the opposite, in fact.

Many members of the public want to get involved with charities. Sometimes the price of admission is prohibitive and, as a result, fundraising events can become exclusive affairs. Empty Bowls is much more accessible for the average person. The ticket price is not restrictive. Attendees can taste soups from several of Toronto's well-known cooks in uniquely crafted bowls donated by potters as a souvenir of the event. Each year representatives from Anishnawbe are on hand to speak about the work they do in the community and to thank everyone for their support. There is a genuine spirit that shines throughout this event—it is difficult to characterize but it feels good.

I have been making soups for many years. Usually people come to the restaurant and perhaps order soup as part of their meal. It always feels good to ladle soup into a bowl for someone. At Empty Bowls, the feeling of giving and sharing and nurturing is heightened. I think all the cooks and potters and organizers of this event share these feelings. We are all grateful for this opportunity to share our talents and to help others in our community.

Jamie Kennedy

The Beginnings

In the early 1990s, ceramic artist John Glick, from Michigan, gave a master class at the Gardiner Museum. He talked about an exciting artists' fundraising project called Empty Bowls. Members of the community would make soup and he and other potters would contribute bowls, to make a kind of *haute* soup kitchen that people would pay to attend. The proceeds went to projects which provided food for those in need. I thought this was a wonderful idea and one that related well to the Gardiner Museum.

In our first Empty Bowls event in 1993, admission was $15 and we had soup from a limited number of chefs. I certainly did not have the nerve to ask the chefs to chauffeur their soup to the museum, nor did I feel that I could ask them to come and serve. So my husband and son-in-law-to-be drove to each of the restaurants and brought the soup to the museum. We then heated batches on the second floor and carried the soup to the first floor where the event was held. What a relief it was in the second year when Jamie Kennedy at JKROM kindly offered to organize the chefs. With Jamie's help, the event became manageable.

The potters responded enthusiastically, with the Mississauga and Thorncliffe Guild of Potters, Clay Design, Sheridan College, Harbourfront Craft Studio and other groups and individuals donating bowls for our paying guests.

Ace Bakery, with its own important philanthropic goals, has generously supplied bread and rolls to this event over the years. Individual musicians, such as Mexican-Canadian guitarist, Jorge López, have entertained the long line of visitors while they waited patiently to select their bowls. We have had so many wonderful contributors in the past decade, they all deserve our gratitude and thanks.

The atmosphere of this event is always special: a sea of happy faces, delighted with their bowls and revelling in the delicious soups and bread. One of the most important moments is when the Anishnawbe Street Patrol drivers and helpers come to talk to us about the individuals they know and respect on the streets and what their work means to them. They invite us to join them on the night-time patrol (giving food, blankets and help) and some of the participants have done just that!

This is the 10th anniversary of Empty Bowls at the Gardiner, an important public program, one that comes from the heart. The spirit of giving, by everyone involved, makes for a poignant and happy occasion.

Susan Jefferies
Curator of Contemporary Ceramics

Foreword

The Gardiner Museum of Ceramic Art in Toronto is home to one of the most exquisite collections of fine porcelain and pottery in the world. The Gardiner is Canada's only public museum dedicated to the collection, exhibition and interpretation of ceramics, and is one of the world's pre-eminent institutions devoted to ceramic art.

While we now admire the beauty of the Gardiner ceramics in their cases, these vessels were really made to serve food and drink. The shape of a pot indicates whether it was used for chocolate, coffee or tea, and the form of a cup also suggests the liquid it was designed to contain. Even the recently translated glyphs on our Maya pieces describe the food they were created to hold. This connection between artifacts and real people's lives is part of what makes the Gardiner collections so appealing. Susan Jefferies understands this appeal, just as she recognized immediately that the combination of delicious soups and beautiful bowls would be impossible for people to resist. This book celebrates a decade of successful Empty Bowls fundraising events at the Gardiner Museum.

Empty Bowls brings Toronto chefs, potters and the public together to raise money for the homeless. The Gardiner provides the venue, participating chefs donate their soup, potters make ceramic bowls, and numerous volunteers donate hours of their time. Members of the public buy tickets that allow them to choose one of the donated bowls to keep and to sample the wonderful soups. All proceeds are given to the Anishnawbe Street Patrol to help the homeless in Toronto.

It is an honour for the Gardiner to participate in such a fine annual event and we are grateful to Susan Jefferies for having had the vision to to make it happen. We are also grateful to long-time supporter Jamie Kennedy, who recruits his fellow chefs, many of whom have contributed to this book; to the talented and most generous potters who donate their bowls; to Ace Bakery; and to Anishnawbe Street Patrol for the essential work they do on our behalf in the community.

Alexandra Montgomery
Director

Message from the Anishnawbe Street Patrol

The Gardiner Museum of Ceramic Art has been a valued supporter of Anishnawbe Health Toronto's Street Patrols Program through its annual fundraising event, Empty Bowls.

Empty Bowls brings together many kind and talented people who demonstrate a generosity towards those in our city who struggle to survive or escape homelessness. The organizers, patrons, artists, chefs and donors truly make Empty Bowls a winner for all. The Street Patrols Program has benefitted greatly from the support of everyone involved.

Our thanks is surpassed only by your generosity.

Joe Hester
Executive Director, Anishnawbe Health Toronto

recipes

Lemon Lentil Soup

SUZANNE BABY

SERVES 4

4 Tbsp. / 60 mL	olive oil
1	large onion, finely diced
1 Tbsp. / 15 mL	fresh garlic, chopped
1 tsp. / 5 mL	ground coriander seed
1/2 tsp. / 2.5 mL	ground cumin seed
1	bay leaf
4 cups / 950 mL	water
1 cup / 240 mL	peeled, seeded, finely diced tomato with juice
1 cup / 240 mL	red lentils, rinsed
	salt and freshly ground black pepper
	spinach leaves chiffonade
	zest of 1/2 lemon
3 Tbsp. / 45 mL	fresh lemon juice (or to taste)

Heat olive oil, add onion and "sweat" gently until translucent. Increase heat, add garlic and sauté for 1 minute. Add ground coriander and cumin. Cook for 1 minute. Add bay leaf, water and tomato. Simmer for 10 minutes. Add lentils. Cook until lentils are tender, about 15 minutes. Season to taste with salt and pepper.

Meanwhile, prepare the spinach. Wash the leaves and discard the stems. To create a chiffonade of the spinach, stack the leaves into small, layered bunches—larger leaves can be rolled tightly if necessary—and slice as finely as possible.

When ready to serve, add the lemon zest, lemon juice and the spinach chiffonade.

Chilled Melon with Port and Lemon Balm Crème Fraîche

SUZANNE BABY

2–3	very ripe cantaloupes, peeled and seeded
1/4 cup / 60 mL	wildflower honey (or to taste)
1–2 cups / 240–475 mL	sparkling mineral water (depending on taste and consistency of melon purée)
1/2 cup / 120 mL	port (or to taste)
4 Tbsp. / 60 mL	crème fraîche
1 tsp. / 5 mL	lemon balm, finely minced

Purée cantaloupes with honey in food processor. Strain. Stir in sparkling water and port to taste. Chill well.

Whip crème fraîche with lemon balm until soft peaks form. Keep chilled.

SERVES 4–6

Port Reduction

1/4–1/2 cup / 60–120 mL	port
1 Tbsp. / 15 mL	sugar

Simmer port gently in a non-reactive saucepan with sugar until syrupy. Chill.

To serve, ladle soup into chilled bowls. Spoon a little lemon crème fraîche into centre of soup. Drizzle lightly with port reduction.

Hot and Sour Duck Broth with Mushrooms

SUZANNE BABY

SERVES 6

4	cloves garlic, crushed
1	2-inch (5-cm) piece fresh ginger, peeled and sliced
1 tsp. / 5 mL	Chinese Five Spice powder
4	pieces star anise
1/2 tsp. / 2.5 mL	chili flakes
6 cups / 1.5 L	duck stock
1/2 cup / 120 mL	mirin
3 Tbsp. / 45 mL	soy sauce
1/4 cup / 60 mL	rice wine vinegar
1/4 cup / 60 mL	white vinegar
	salt and freshly ground black pepper to taste
1/4 cup / 60 mL	shiitake mushrooms, stemmed, roasted and thinly sliced
1/8 cup / 30 mL	Chinese dried "pine needle" mushrooms, soaked and shredded
1/8 cup / 30 mL	carrot, finely julienned
1/4 package	fresh enoki mushrooms
1/8 cup / 30 mL	firm tofu, diced
2	green onions, slivered

TIP

To make duck stock, substitute duck bones for chicken bones in any chicken stock recipe (see page 122).

Wrap the garlic, ginger, Chinese Five Spice powder, star anise and chili flakes in cheesecloth to make a spice bag. To infuse the duck stock with the spices, simmer together for 20–30 minutes. Remove spice bag. Add mirin, soy sauce and both vinegars. Check and adjust sweet and sour flavours, seasoning with salt and pepper. Add shiitake and pine needle mushrooms and simmer for 5 minutes. Add carrot and simmer for 1 minute. Add enoki mushrooms, tofu and green onion. Serve immediately.

Charred Eggplant Soup with Spiced Chickpeas

For the soup

SUZANNE BABY

4	medium, firm eggplant
1	onion, chopped
4 Tbsp. / 60 mL	olive oil
3 Tbsp. / 45 mL	fresh garlic, chopped
1 cup / 240 mL	dry white wine
6 cups / 950 mL	chicken stock or water
	salt and freshly ground black pepper
4 Tbsp. / 60 mL	extra-virgin olive oil
2 Tbsp. / 30 mL	lemon juice

SERVES 6

Preheat grill or barbecue. Char eggplant until flesh is completely soft and skin is blackened and brittle. Cool. Peel and discard skin. Reserve cooled flesh.

In a Dutch oven or large saucepan, sauté onion in olive oil until soft. Add garlic and sauté for 1 minute. Add wine, chicken stock or water, and eggplant. Simmer for 20–30 minutes until eggplant is tender. Purée in a food processor or blender and strain. Season with salt and pepper. Keep warm. Prepare chickpeas.

When ready to serve, blend extra-virgin olive oil and lemon juice into purée.

For the chickpeas

1/4 cup / 60 mL	cooked chickpeas
1 Tbsp. / 15 mL	red onion, finely chopped
1/2 tsp. / 2.5 mL	ground coriander seed
1/8 tsp. / .5 mL	ground turmeric
1/2 tsp. / 2.5 mL	ground anise seed
1/8 tsp. / .5 mL	ground fennel seed
pinch	chili flakes
1	1-inch (2.5-cm) piece fresh ginger, grated
1 Tbsp. / 15 mL	extra-virgin olive oil
1 Tbsp. / 15 mL	lemon juice
1 Tbsp. / 15 mL	chopped fresh coriander
	salt and freshly ground black pepper

Toss ingredients together. Check seasoning. To serve, ladle soup into bowls. Spoon chickpeas into the centre of each bowl.

Chilled Sugar Snap Pea Soup with Marinated Scallops

SUZANNE BABY

For the scallops

1 Tbsp. / 15 mL	extra-virgin olive oil
10–12	small (or 4–6 large) bay scallops
1 Tbsp. / 15 mL	lime juice
1/2 tsp. / 2.5 mL	lime zest
	salt and freshly ground black pepper

Dice scallops very finely. Toss with olive oil, lime juice and zest. Season to taste. Keep refrigerated until ready to serve.

SERVES 6

For the soup

1	large onion, diced
1–2 Tbsp. / 15–30 mL	vegetable oil
1 Tbsp. / 15 mL	sugar
1 cup / 240 mL	dry white wine
6 cups / 950 mL	chicken stock or water
1	bay leaf
4	sprigs fresh thyme, tied in string
	salt and freshly ground black pepper to taste
1 1/2 lbs. / 880 g	sugar snap peas

Heat the olive oil over medium-high heat. Add the onion and sweat gently until translucent and very soft. Add the sugar and cook for 1 minute. Add the wine and simmer for 5–10 minutes. Add the chicken stock or water, bay leaf and thyme sprigs. Simmer for 20 minutes.

Prepare a large container of ice water.

Strain soup base, discarding onion, bay leaf and thyme sprigs. Return strained stock to a boil. Add 1 tsp. (5 mL) salt. To blanch peas, add to the boiling stock, cooking until they just begin to soften. Strain out peas immediately—retaining stock—and plunge quickly in ice water to cool. Drain as soon as they have cooled. Chill the reserved stock. When cold, purée peas with stock. Strain. Season with salt and pepper.

To serve, ladle soup into chilled bowls. Spoon scallops into the centre of each bowl.

Gary Hoyer's Vegetable Stock

Almost all good soups start with a carefully made stock. Vegetable stock doesn't need a long time to make, so if I'm making a nice soup for company, say, I might start my stock before I do a quick tidy, let it simmer away while I'm preparing dinner, and have it hot and ready to add to the rest of the soup ingredients once they're ready for it.

LAUREN BOYINGTON

MAKES 6 QUARTS (6 L)

2 Tbsp / 30 mL	vegetable oil
4	medium onions, sliced
2	cloves garlic, sliced
3	carrots, sliced
$1/2$	head celery, sliced
1	leek, trimmed, sliced, and well rinsed
1	small celery root, well scrubbed, sliced
24 cups / 6 L	water
1	handful fresh herbs (your preference)
2–3	tomatoes, canned or fresh
1 tsp. / 5 mL	black peppercorns
1	bay leaf
1	clove

Heat oil in a 40-cup (10-L) stockpot over medium-low heat. Add onions, garlic, carrots, celery, leek and celery root and sauté until cooked through, about 10 minutes. Add the water, herbs, tomatoes, peppercorns, bay leaf and clove. Bring to a boil over moderate heat, skim and simmer for 20 minutes. Strain.

Bean Soup with Smoked Sun-Dried Tomatoes and Herbed Quark

LAUREN BOYINGTON

Smoked sun-dried tomatoes are an especially valuable ingredient in the vegetarian repertoire because of their smokey flavour. If you can't get them (they're in limited supply), consider substituting smoked dried mushrooms, dried or canned chipotle peppers, or a couple of tablespoons of grated smoked cheese swirled into each bowl before adding the herbed quark.

SERVES 8

1/2 cup / 120 mL	each of any 3 of your favourite dried beans (except split pea and dahl lentils), picked over and rinsed separately
5	cloves garlic, minced
2 Tbsp. / 30 mL	olive oil
2	medium onions, finely diced
3	stalks celery, finely diced
2	carrots, finely diced
1/4 tsp. / 1.2 mL	chili flakes
8	smoked sun-dried tomatoes, soaked, drained and chopped
16 cups / 4 L	Gary Hoyer's Vegetable Stock (page 19)
	sea salt and freshly ground black pepper
1	bay leaf
4 cups / 500 mL	Quark
1/2 cup / 120 mL	fresh herbs of your choice, finely chopped
	root vegetable chips, for garnish

Soak the 3 varieties of beans in separate containers overnight.

Rinse beans, and cook in separate pots, in cold, unsalted water. Bring to a boil and skim, reduce heat and simmer until tender but not mushy. Drain.

Sauté garlic in olive oil until golden. Add onions and sauté until translucent. Add celery, carrots and chili flakes and sauté until the vegetables are almost cooked through. Add the cooked beans, sun-dried tomatoes and vegetable stock. Season with salt and pepper. Add bay leaf. Bring to a boil, skim, reduce heat and simmer for 20 minutes.

Adjust seasoning before serving.

To garnish, mix Quark with herbs, season with salt and pepper, and spoon into the middle of each bowl of soup. Stud island with vegetable chips, add a sprig of one of the herbs you are using, and the only thing missing is a miniature Muskoka chair!

P.S. Whoever gets the bay leaf has to help with the dishes.

Sweet Potato and Red Lentil Soup

LAUREN BOYINGTON

You can get all the ingredients for this soup in any East Indian store. Chat masala is a mixture of spices and dried mango, sold in small boxes. Tamarind is available in jars as a paste, and also as a compressed cake. The paste must be diluted with hot water to a jam-like consistency; the cake must be soaked and then pressed through a sieve to separate the seeds from the pulp. Worth the bother, in either case.

SERVES 8

1^1/$_2$ cups / 360 mL	red dahl lentils, picked over and rinsed
3	large sweet potatoes
2 Tbsp. / 30 mL	vegetable oil
5	cloves garlic, finely minced
2	medium onions, chopped
2 Tbsp. / 30 mL	coriander seed
1 Tbsp. / 15 mL	cumin seeds
1 tsp. / 5 mL	fenugreek
1	cinnamon stick
^{1}/$_2$–1 tsp. / 2.5–5 mL	dried chilies
	chat masala
3	medium carrots, diced
4	stalks celery, diced
^{1}/$_4$ cup / 60 mL	fresh ginger, finely chopped
12 cups / 3 L	Gary Hoyer's Vegetable Stock (page 19)
2	ripe mangos, peeled and diced
2 Tbsp. / 30 mL	tamarind purée
	brown sugar to taste
2	shallots, finely diced, soaked in the juice of 1 lime
	cilantro
1	bunch green onion
1–2	fresh chilies, finely chopped
	sea salt and freshly ground black pepper
	sev

Soak lentils overnight in cold water.

Wash and dry sweet potatoes. Rub with oil and roast at 350°F (175°C) until soft, about 40 minutes. Cool, peel and roughly chop.

Pour about 2 Tbsp. (30 mL) of oil into a large frying pan and heat on medium. Fry garlic in the oil, stirring until the garlic is golden and smells sweet. Immediately add the onions, and sauté until translucent. Toast the coriander, cumin and fenugreek under a medium-high broiler. Watch carefully and remove immediately when the seeds begin to darken in colour. Grind with a mortar and pestle. Add the coriander, cumin, fenugreek, cinnamon, dried chilies and chat masala. Add carrots, celery and ginger and sweat until almost soft.

Drain soaked lentils and add to the vegetables. Add enough vegetable stock to cover and cook lentils at a slow simmer for about 45 minutes, or until they are completely broken down and have a sweet taste. (Add more vegetable stock if necessary, and give the pot a stir from time to time to make sure that nothing is sticking to the bottom.) Add roasted sweet potato and 8 cups (2 L) of vegetable stock, bring to a boil, skim and simmer for 20 minutes. Purée with a hand blender.

Garnish
Combine mangos with tamarind, brown sugar, shallots, cilantro, green onion and fresh chilies. Season with salt and pepper.

Serve soup with a good handful of sev and a dollop of mango mixture. Serve the rest of the sev in a bowl on the side, as your guests may want more.

Swirled Purées of Green Pea and Yukon Gold Potato

LAUREN BOYINGTON

SERVES 10

2	medium onions, diced
2	cloves garlic, finely minced
2 Tbsp. / 30 mL	vegetable oil
3	stalks celery, diced
5	medium Yukon Gold potatoes, cut into large dice
1	medium celery root, well scrubbed and peeled, cut into large dice
16 cups / 4 L	Gary Hoyer's Vegetable Stock (page 19)
1	bay leaf
1	sprig fresh thyme
1/2 cup / 120 mL	35% cream
4 cups / 950 mL	frozen green peas
1	bunch leeks, cleaned, trimmed and diced
3	sprigs fresh rosemary, leaves only, finely chopped
1	bunch parsley, finely chopped
1	bunch chervil, finely chopped
	sea salt and freshly ground black pepper

For the potato soup

Sauté one onion and one clove of garlic in half the oil until translucent. Add half the celery and sweat. Add potatoes and celery root and 8 cups (2 L) of vegetable stock, along with the bay leaf and a sprig of fresh thyme. Bring to a boil, reduce heat and simmer until vegetables are tender, adding more stock if necessary. Remove bay leaf and thyme, purée and pour through a strainer into another pot. Stir in some cream, reserving some to adjust the consistency as needed.

For the pea soup

Follow the above procedure with the reserved onion, garlic, oil, celery and bunch of leeks. Add frozen peas, stir briefly to combine, and add 4 1/4 cups (1 L) of vegetable stock, rosemary, salt and pepper. Bring to a boil, skim and remove from heat. Add parsley and chervil, purée and pass through a strainer into another pot.

Adjust consistency of the two purées with remaining hot stock (it's important that they not be too thin). Adjust seasoning. Reheat briefly and ladle both soups into bowls so that they swirl together. Too pretty to garnish, really.

Chilled Melon with Port and Lemon Balm
Crème Fraîche   p. 15

BOWL BY KATHY THOMPSON

Black Bean and Double-Smoked Bacon Soup
with Lime Coriander Sour Cream   p. 26

BOWL BY JENNIFER FULLER

Mushroom Consommé with Enoki Mushroom
and Green Onion Garnish   p. 35

BOWL BY MARY WHITE

Mussel Soup with Saffron and Thyme   p. 27

BOWL BY MARNI LOCKINGTON

Lamb and Tomato Soup with
Fava Beans and Gremolata

KEITH FROGGETT

2 Tbsp. / 30 mL	olive oil
2 lbs. / 900 g	lamb shanks
2	stalks celery, diced
2	red onions, chopped
2	carrots, diced
4	large tomatoes, peeled, seeded and diced, juice reserved
1 Tbsp. / 15 mL	balsamic vinegar
12	cloves garlic
4	sprigs fresh parsley
4	sprigs fresh thyme
	water
1 lb. / 450 g	fresh fava beans, shelled, blanched and shelled again
	extra-virgin olive oil
1 recipe	Gremolata (see below)

SERVES 4

Heat the olive oil in a large pot and brown the lamb shanks all over. Remove. Add the celery, onions and carrots and brown lightly. Add the tomato juice, the diced tomato and vinegar. Place the garlic cloves, parsley and thyme in a piece of cheesecloth to make a bundle and tie it with string. Put the garlic-herb bundle in the pot, place the shanks on top and cover with water. Bring to boiling point, then reduce heat to a bare simmer. Cook for about 2 hours, then remove garlic-herb bundle. Increase heat and boil for 15 minutes, skimming as required. The meat should be "fall-off-the-bone" tender.

Pull the shank meat from the bone, then return the meat to the soup along with the fava beans. Adjust the seasoning and flavour with extra-virgin olive oil and gremolata.

Gremolata

4 Tbsp. / 60 mL	chopped parsley
1	clove garlic, chopped
	zest of 1/2 lemon

Mix well and sprinkle over soup.

Black Bean and Double-Smoked Bacon Soup with Lime Coriander Sour Cream

KEITH FROGGETT

1 tsp. / 5 mL	unsalted butter
1/2 lb. / 225 g	double-smoked bacon, diced
1	large onion, sliced
2 cups / 475 mL	dry black turtle beans, washed well
4–6 cups / 1–1.5 L	chicken stock
	salt and freshly ground black pepper
1 recipe	Lime Coriander Sour Cream (see below)
1/2 cup / 120 mL	tomato, finely diced

SERVES 6

In a large soup pot, melt the butter then sweat the bacon and onion in it for a few moments. Add the beans and cover with stock. Simmer until beans are soft, adding more stock as needed.

Strain the beans, onion and bacon from the liquid. Reserve the liquid for now. Purée the bean mixture in a food processor—working in batches if necessary—until smooth. Add just enough of the liquid to give a smooth, velvety texture. Transfer the purée to a clean soup pot. Adjust the seasoning.

Lime Coriander Sour Cream

1/2 cup / 120 mL	sour cream
3 Tbsp. / 45 mL	fresh lime juice
1 Tbsp. / 15 mL	chopped fresh coriander

Mix the sour cream with the lime juice. Stir in a good amount of coriander.

To serve, reheat the soup then drizzle over the Lime Coriander Sour Cream and garnish with finely diced tomato.

Mussel Soup with Saffron and Thyme

KEITH FROGGETT

2 lbs. / 900 g	cultivated mussels
1	bunch fresh thyme
3	egg yolks
7 oz. / 200 mL	35% cream
6 Tbsp. / 85 mL	unsalted butter
1	large onion, thinly sliced
1 cup / 240 mL	dry white wine
1	leek, julienned
1	carrot, julienned
1	stalk celery, julienned
pinch	saffron
	salt and freshly ground black pepper

SERVES 4

Wash the mussels and remove any of the beard-like hairs that often protrude from their shells.

Wash the thyme and remove the leaves from the stalks. Reserve the thyme stems and chop the leaves. Whisk the egg yolks and cream together. Set aside. Heat 5 Tbsp. (75 mL) of the butter in a large pot with a close-fitting lid. Add the onions and thyme stalks. Sauté gently for a few moments, add the mussels and wine. Cover and cook over high heat. Shake the pan after a few minutes so that the mussels on the bottom go to the top. When all the mussels have opened, drain them in a colander set over a bowl to catch all the juices. Remove the mussels from the shells. Strain the liquid through a cheesecloth and put in a clean saucepan, bring to a boil.

In another pan, gently sweat the leeks, carrots and celery with the saffron in the remaining butter for a few moments. Add 1 Tbsp. (15 mL) of chopped thyme leaves and then pour in the boiling stock. Add the mussels and the cream and egg yolk mixture. Whisking all the time, bring back to the boil and remove from the heat immediately.

Season and serve.

Pumpkin and Peanut Butter Soup

BETSY GUTNIK

This recipe was given to me by a friend who had spent a lot of time in North Africa, where they use a lot of peanut butter in their cooking.

2 tsp. / 10 mL	olive oil
2 tsp. / 10 mL	garlic, finely chopped
1 cup / 240 mL	onion, finely chopped
1/2 cup / 120 mL	carrot, finely chopped
1/2 cup / 120 mL	celery, finely chopped
3 1/2 cups / 840 mL	chicken or vegetable stock
1	14 oz. (398 mL) can pumpkin
1	8 oz. (227 mL) can white kidney beans
1	bay leaf
1 tsp. / 5 mL	ground ginger
1/4 cup / 60 mL	smooth peanut butter
	salt and freshly ground black pepper
	fresh coriander or Italian parsley

SERVES 4

In a medium stockpot, heat olive oil and gently sauté garlic, onion, carrot and celery until soft. Add stock, pumpkin, beans, bay leaf, ginger and peanut butter, and bring to a boil. Reduce heat to a gentle simmer and cook for about 15 minutes or until all vegetables are soft. Remove bay leaf and season with salt and pepper. (Note: Sugar may be added to sweeten the taste.)

Serve with a nice garnish of chopped coriander or Italian parsley.

Spring Carrot and Cardamom Soup

This recipe works best with young, sweet spring carrots, but you may substitute regular bunched carrots. It will still be good.

BETSY GUTNIK

1 tsp. / 5 mL	olive oil
1	shallot, finely chopped
1¹/₄ lbs. / 565 g	spring carrots, peeled and sliced
3¹/₂ cups / 840 mL	vegetable or chicken stock
1 tsp. / 5 mL	harissa paste
15–20	cardamom seeds, crushed
2	large oranges, juiced
1 tsp. / 5 mL	orange zest
	salt
	plain yogurt, for garnish
	harissa paste, for garnish

SERVES 4

In a medium stockpot, heat the olive oil on meduim heat and sauté the shallot until translucent. Add the carrots and stock and bring to a boil. Add the harissa, cardamom, orange juice and zest, and lightly season with salt. Simmer until carrots are soft, about 15 minutes. Remove from heat and cool slightly.

In a food processor, purée the mixture until smooth. Taste and adjust seasoning. Serve, garnished with a dollop of yogurt and a swirl of harissa paste.

Roasted Red Pepper Soup with Polenta Croutons

BETSY GUTNIK

Roasted pepper soup is always a favourite—the garnish is its selling feature. Here is where I pull out all the "chef" stops.

SERVES 4

2 Tbsp. / 30 mL	olive oil
1 cup / 240 mL	onion, finely chopped
1 cup / 240 mL	potato, peeled and sliced
2 Tbsp. / 30 mL	garlic, finely chopped
1 Tbsp. / 15 mL	tomato paste
4	red peppers, roasted, peeled, seeded and chopped
1	bay leaf
4 cups / 1 L	vegetable stock
	balsamic vinegar to taste
	salt and freshly ground black pepper

In a medium stockpot, heat the olive oil and sauté the onion, potato and garlic until slightly brown. Stir in the tomato paste and cook for 1 minute. Add the red peppers, bay leaf and stock and bring to a boil. Reduce heat and simmer gently for 25 minutes. Remove bay leaf and let cool slightly.

In a food processor, purée the mixture until smooth. Add balsamic vinegar and salt and pepper. Serve at once.

Polenta Croutons

3 cups / 720 mL	vegetable stock or water
1 tsp. / 5 mL	unsalted butter
1 tsp. / 5 mL	salt
1 cup / 240 mL	coarse cornmeal
3 Tbsp. / 45 mL	olive oil
	salt

In a heavy saucepan, bring stock or water and butter to a boil. Add salt and cornmeal in a steady stream, stirring with a wooden spoon. Reduce the heat and cook mixture for a few more minutes, stirring constantly. As the mixture thickens, place on a parchment-covered baking sheet. Spread mixture flat, using a palette knife dipped in cold water. Cool until very firm. Cut into desired size and shape.

In a sauté pan, heat the olive oil. Sauté the croutons until lightly browned. Remove from pan and place on paper towel to dry. Lightly salt to taste.

Berlin Potato Soup

BETSY GUTNIK

Serve this soup with a crusty baguette, Leonard Cohen in the background and a good Riesling wine. I recommend Thirty Bench Late Harvest from Jordan, Ontario.

6 oz. / 175 g	smoked back bacon, fat removed, diced
10 oz. / 300 g	Yukon Gold potatoes, peeled and diced
1	onion, finely chopped
4 cups / 1 L	chicken stock
1 tsp. / 5 mL	fresh marjoram, finely chopped (or 1/2 tsp./2.5 mL dried marjoram)
1 cup / 240 mL	carrots, diced
1 cup / 240 mL	celery root, diced
1	leek, white part only, diced
1 cup / 240 mL	35% cream
	salt and freshly ground black pepper

SERVES 4

Sauté bacon in a stockpot until cooked through, about 5 minutes. Add potatoes and onion, and sauté until onion is translucent. Add stock and marjoram and simmer for 25 minutes. Add carrots, celery root and leek, and cook for an additional 10 minutes. Remove from heat and purée the mixture in a food processor. Add cream and season with salt and pepper.

(Note: Check flavour before adding additional salt as bacon will increase the salt content of the mixture.)

Asparagus Soup   p. 47

BOWL BY LUCIE RIE

Cauliflower Soup with Spinach
and Indian Spices   p. 37

BOWL BY BILL REDDICK

Poitou-Style Fresh Pea
Soup   p. 39

BOWL BY MARC LEMIEUX

Roasted Onion Soup   p. 46

BOWL BY SHEILA CAPLAN

Kohlrabi Soup

Unique and delicious!

BETSY GUTNIK

1 oz. / 28 g	unsalted butter
2	kohlrabi, peeled and cubed
1	small Yukon Gold potato, peeled and cubed
1 Tbsp. / 15 mL	onion, finely diced
1–2 Tbsp. / 15–30 mL	flour
5 cups / 1.2 L	brown stock
	pinch freshly ground nutmeg
	salt and freshly ground black pepper
3 Tbsp. / 45 mL	35% cream
1 Tbsp. / 15 mL	finely chopped fresh parsley

SERVES 4

Heat butter in stockpot until melted. Add kohlrabi, potato and onion, and sauté until onion is translucent. Sprinkle with flour and sauté until brown. Add stock and nutmeg, and season with salt and pepper. Simmer until vegetables are tender, 15–20 minutes. Remove from heat and purée in a food processor until smooth. Stir in cream and parsley.

Zuppa Rustica

LINDA HAYNES

4	slices bacon, chopped
3 Tbsp. / 45 mL	onion, finely chopped
4	slices sourdough or country bread, sliced 3/4 inch (1.9 cm) thick
6 cups / 1.5 L	chicken stock
2 Tbsp. / 30 mL	Dijon mustard
1	bay leaf
1 cup / 240 mL	homogenized milk
	salt
pinch	freshly ground black pepper
	parsley, for garnish

SERVES 6

Sauté the bacon over medium-low heat for about 5 minutes, until some of the fat is rendered but the bacon is still soft. Add onion and continue cooking for about 8 minutes until onion is soft and barely golden. Drain the bacon and onion on paper towel and pat off any extra grease.

Toast the bread under the broiler until it is dark golden brown but not burned. Cut into 1-inch (2.5-cm) cubes.

Heat stock and add the bacon/onion mixture, bread, mustard and bay leaf. Simmer covered for 15 minutes. Remove the bay leaf and add milk. Purée in batches in a food processor. Add salt and pepper to taste.

Heat and serve in large cups with a parsley sprig as garnish.

For an unusual and very modern presentation, froth 1 cup (240 mL) of the soup and gently spoon a bit of it on top of each cup.

Mushroom Consommé with Enoki Mushroom and Green Onion Garnish

LINDA HAYNES

This soup was inspired by a vegetable stew cooked by Gordon Hammersley of Hammersley's Bistro in Boston, Massachusetts. The consommé is fat free but its flavourful, satisfying taste belies that. Serve it with plenty of warm baguette.

2	large portobello mushrooms, with stems
2 lbs. / 900 g	white button mushrooms
2 Tbsp. / 30 mL	chopped garlic
1	large Spanish onion, chopped
1 cup / 240 mL	dried porcini mushrooms
3 1/2 cups / 840 mL	dry white wine
12 cups / 3 L	water
1 cup / 240 mL	soy sauce
1/4 tsp. / 1.2 mL	salt
2 tsp. / 10 mL	fresh thyme leaves

SERVES 10

Scrape the gills out of the portobello mushrooms. Finely chop the white and portobello mushrooms.

Heat a heavy-bottomed stockpot large enough to hold all the ingredients over high heat for 2–3 minutes. It is imperative that the pot be very hot before you add the mushrooms. Add the button and portobello mushrooms, garlic and onions and cook, stirring, for about 5 minutes until the mushrooms release their water. Don't be concerned if some of the mushroom mixture sticks to the bottom of the pot when you first start cooking it.

Meanwhile, wash the porcinis and drain through a coffee filter to remove any sand residue. Add the porcini mushrooms, wine, water, soy sauce, salt and thyme and bring to a boil. Remove from stovetop, cover and let sit for 45 minutes. Return to stove and simmer, still covered, for another 45 minutes.

Pour the broth through a fine strainer twice. Reserve 3 cups (720 mL) of the mushroom mixture. Spoon 2 Tbsp. (30 mL) of mushroom mixture into individual heated bowls. Ladle 1 1/2 cups (360 mL) of broth into each bowl and garnish with a few enoki mushrooms and some green onion rings.

Garnish
1 package enoki mushrooms, washed and trimmed

3 green onions, green part only, finely sliced into rings

Ten-Minute Soup

LINDA HAYNES

This quick soup depends on good chicken broth. It's a simple but nourishing recipe that looks beautiful and tastes light.

9 cups / 2.3 L	strong chicken broth
6	¹/₂-inch (1.2-cm) slices of rustic white or country bread
6	eggs
6 Tbsp. / 90 mL	grated Parmigiano-Reggiano cheese
6 tsp. / 30 mL	minced Italian parsley

SERVES 6

Bring the broth to a simmer. Cut each slice of bread to fit the bottom of your bowls. Toast.

Poach the eggs. They can be poached just ahead of time and held on a dry tea towel until ready to serve.

Place a slice of toast in each of 6 heated bowls. Ladle 1¹/₂ cups (360 mL) of broth into each bowl. Carefully slide 1 egg into each bowl. Sprinkle 1 Tbsp. (15 mL) of cheese and 1 tsp. (5 mL) of parsley over each egg.

Cauliflower Soup with Spinach and Indian Spices

LINDA HAYNES

If you think Indian means spicy you'll be surprised at the fragrant, subtle flavourings of this soup. I love the saffron colour the turmeric gives to it and the spinach leaves turn a brilliant, glossy green. Try serving it with baked tortilla chips, grilled country bread drizzled with good olive oil or cornbread (page 40).

3 Tbsp. / 45 mL	corn, vegetable or canola oil
6	green cardamom seeds
2 tsp. / 10 mL	ground coriander (the flavour will be fresher if you grind your own)
1 tsp. / 5 mL	ground turmeric
pinch	cayenne
1/2 cup / 120 mL	onion, finely chopped
2	cloves garlic, minced
1	head cauliflower (about 1 to 1 1/2 lbs. / 565 to 680 g), coarsely chopped
2	medium Yukon Gold potatoes, cut in 1/4-inch (.6-cm) dice
1 Tbsp. / 15 mL	Dijon mustard
6–7 cups / 1.5–1.8 L	light chicken stock
2 tsp. / 10 mL	salt
	freshly ground white pepper
1	very large handful washed baby spinach
	yogurt, for garnish

MAKES ABOUT 12 CUPS
(3L)

Heat oil in a pot large enough to accommodate all the ingredients. Add cardamom seeds and sauté about 1 minute until they give up their oils. Take seeds out of oil and discard them. Lower heat to medium-low and add coriander, turmeric and cayenne. Sauté for about 20 seconds until you can smell the spices.

(continued on next page)

Add the onion and garlic. Sauté for about 5 minutes, or until the onions are wilted. Lower the heat if the onions start to brown. Add the cauliflower, potatoes and mustard. Toss until the spices coat the vegetables and sauté for 2–3 minutes until the vegetables are slightly roasted.

Pour in 6 cups (1.5 L) of stock and simmer, covered, for 20–30 minutes or until vegetables are soft.

If you have time cool the mixture, purée it in a food processor. Add salt and pepper to taste.

If you find the purée too thick add the extra cup of stock.

Reheat and taste for seasonings. Stir in spinach just before serving. It will turn bright green and have a slight crunch.

Pour into bowls and garnish with a dollop of yogurt.

This soup can be made ahead to the point where you add the spinach. It will keep in the fridge for 5 days or in the freezer for 6 months.

Poitou-Style Fresh Pea Soup

The French province of Poitou-Charentes is located in the mid-west of France. As well as being the inspiration for this soup, it is also known for its Cognac, pottery and chocolates.

LINDA HAYNES

SERVES 6 HOT (8 COLD)

3 Tbsp. / 45 mL	unsalted butter
1 1/2 cups / 360 mL	onions, thinly sliced
5 cups / 1.2 L	shelled fresh or frozen peas
1 1/2 tsp. / 7.5 mL	fresh thyme, chopped
1 1/2 tsp. / 7.5 mL	fresh savoury, chopped
3 Tbsp. / 45 mL	fresh parsley, chopped
1 1/2 tsp. / 7.5 mL	sugar
3 cups / 720 mL	lightly packed Boston lettuce, roughly chopped
6 cups / 1.5 L	chicken or vegetable stock (add 1 to 2 cups/240 to 475 mL more if serving cold)
3/4 tsp. / 4 mL	salt
1/4 tsp. / 1.2 mL	white pepper
1/4 cup / 60 mL	fresh ricotta
6	slices white baguette (8 slices if serving cold)
2 Tbsp. / 30 mL	walnuts, finely chopped

Heat butter in a saucepan large enough to hold all the ingredients. Add onions and sweat until softened but not browned, 5–8 minutes. Add peas, herbs, sugar and lettuce and toss until coated. Pour in stock, salt and pepper. Cover and simmer until peas are just cooked, about 20 minutes.

Purée in batches in a food processor. If you want a perfectly smooth soup pour it through a sieve or food mill, pressing on the solids.

To make the crostini spread 2 tsp. (10 mL) of ricotta on each slice of baguette and top with some chopped walnuts. Toast in a toaster oven or in the oven until the bread is crisped.

Pour the soup into the bowls and float 1 crostini on top of each bowl of soup. If serving cold, place soup in fridge for at least 2 hours. The starches in the peas will make the soup solid. Add one additional stock to get the desired consistency. Top with a crostini if you wish.

Cornbread

Ten minutes of preparation time and 15 minutes in the oven. It doesn't get much easier than this. The buttermilk gives the cornbread a nice, rich flavour even though it's very low in fat.

MAKES 1 ROUND LOAF

1 cup / 240 mL	cake flour
1 1/4 cups / 300 mL	cornmeal
4 tsp. / 20 mL	baking powder
1 tsp. / 5 mL	salt
1	egg
1 3/4 cups / 420 mL	buttermilk
1/4 tsp. / 1.2 mL	hot chili powder
6 Tbsp. / 90 mL	unsalted butter, melted and brought to room temperature
1 1/2 cups / 360 mL	corn kernels from about 2 cobs (or frozen and defrosted corn)
1 tsp. / 5 mL	green jalapeño pepper, seeded and minced
1 Tbsp. / 15 mL	vegetable oil

Preheat an oven to 425°F (220°C). Place an 8–10 inch (20–25 cm) iron skillet in the oven while mixing the batter.

In a medium bowl, sift the flour, cornmeal, baking powder and salt together. In a small bowl, lightly whisk the egg and the buttermilk together. Pour the buttermilk mixture into the flour mixture and stir with a wooden spoon until blended. Sprinkle the chili powder into the butter and mix into the batter. Stir in the corn and the jalapeño.

Carefully remove the hot skillet from the oven, and place on the stove over high heat. Pour the vegetable oil into the skillet. When it is heated and easily coats the bottom of the skillet, add the batter and smooth the top. Turn heat down to medium and cook for about 1 minute; this will give the cornbread a nice crust. If you prefer a softer outer crust, take the skillet off the heat immediately. In either case, return the skillet to the oven for about 15 minutes. Test with a cake skewer and remove from oven. The cornbread should rest in the skillet for 5 minutes before you turn it out.

Cut into pie-shaped wedges and serve warm.

Mulligatawny

GARY HOYER

1	whole chicken, about 3 lbs. (1.5 kg)
10 cups / 2.4 L	water
2 tsp. / 10 mL	salt
1/2 tsp. / 2.5 mL	peppercorns
	handful celery leaves
4	medium onions, chopped
4	cloves
1 Tbsp. / 15 mL	coriander seed, roasted and ground (see page 23)
1/2 Tbsp. / 7.5 mL	cumin seed, roasted and ground (see page 23)
1 tsp. / 5 mL	fennel seed, roasted and ground (see page 23)
1/2 tsp. / 2.5 mL	turmeric
4	cloves garlic
1 Tbsp. / 15 mL	fresh ginger, grated
1	2-inch (5-cm) cinnamon stick
2 Tbsp. / 30 mL	ghee or clarified butter
12	dried curry leaves
1 1/2 lbs. / 680 g	fresh tomatoes, chopped
1 cup / 240 mL	thick coconut milk
	lemon juice
	sea salt and freshly ground black pepper

SERVES 6

In a stockpot cook the chicken with the water, salt and pepper, celery leaves and half the onions. Bring to boiling point, reduce heat and simmer for 1 hour. Add the spices in the last half hour of cooking. Strain, reserving stock. Cool chicken. Shred meat and reserve for soup. Fry remaining onion in ghee or butter till golden, add curry leaves and tomatoes and fry. Add reserved chicken stock, boil, then simmer for a few minutes. Add reserved meat. Add coconut milk and remove from heat. Add lemon, adjust seasoning and serve with rice or stringhoppers.

TIP
Instead of using store-bought ghee, clarify butter by heating it until it melts and stops bubbling. Allow to cool so that salt and sediment sink to bottom of pan. Pour off the fat and strain through muslin or cheesecloth.

Hot and Sour Soup

GARY HOYER

SERVES 6

4 Tbsp. / 60 mL	red pepper, finely chopped
2 Tbsp. / 30 mL	vegetable oil
4 Tbsp. / 60 mL	fresh tomato, finely chopped
1¹⁄₂ Tbsp. / 22.5 mL	garlic, chopped
¹⁄₂ cup / 120 mL	leeks, white part only, chopped
2 Tbsp. / 30 mL	shallot, diced
1 Tbsp./ 15 mL	fresh ginger, grated
¹⁄₂	fresh chili pepper, finely chopped
1 Tbsp. / 15 mL	corn flour
8 cups / 2 L	pork and/or chicken stock
2 oz. / 57 g	cellophane noodles, cut into 1-inch (2.5-cm) pieces
2 cups / 475 mL	cooked pork, cut into julienne
6	dry shiitake and black wood ear mushrooms, soaked, cleaned and sliced
2 Tbsp. / 30 mL	tomato sauce
1 Tbsp. / 15 mL	soy sauce
1¹⁄₂ Tbsp. / 22.5 mL	rice vinegar
2 tsp. / 10 mL	sesame oil
3 Tbsp. / 45 mL	pickled turnip
1	egg, beaten
	sea salt and freshly ground black pepper
2	scallions, finely chopped
2 Tbsp. / 30 mL	lemon zest, minced
1¹⁄₂ Tbsp. / 22.5 mL	fresh coriander, finely chopped
1 cup / 240 mL	tofu, cubed

Choose a Dutch oven or stockpot. Sauté pepper in half the vegetable oil for 1 minute, add fresh tomato and sauté 1 minute. Remove. In the remaining oil, sauté garlic until light golden. Add leeks and sweat until soft; add shallot and sweat 1 minute; add ginger and chili and fry 1 minute.

Blend the corn flour with a little of the stock and reserve. Add the rest of stock and bring to boiling, add slurry of corn flour and blend well. Add noodles, pork, mushrooms, tomato sauce, soy sauce, rice vinegar, sesame oil and turnip. Reduce heat. Simmer 10 minutes. Add egg and gently whisk in to create strands. Adjust seasoning. Finish by adding scallion, lemon, coriander and tofu. Add more chili or vinegar to taste if desired.

Bean Soup Harira

1½ cups / 360 mL	dried white beans
⅔ cup / 160 mL	dried chickpeas
½ cup / 120 mL	lentils
2	onions, 1 clove-studded, 1 chopped
½ cup / 120 mL	cloves garlic
1 Tbsp. / 15 mL	cumin
1 Tbsp. / 15 mL	coriander seed
1 Tbsp. / 15 mL	paprika
pinch	saffron
1 tsp. / 5 mL	ground cinnamon
2 Tbsp. / 30 mL	unsalted butter
⅓ cup / 80 mL	fresh ginger, finely minced
1 tsp. / 5 mL	ground turmeric
2 cups / 475 mL	fresh plum tomatoes, chopped
8 cups / 2 L	vegetable stock
8 cups / 2 L	bean liquor
2 Tbsp. / 30 mL	chopped flat parsley
4 Tbsp. / 60 mL	chopped fresh cilantro
¼ cup / 60 mL	fresh lemon juice
2	eggs
	sea salt and freshly ground pepper

GARY HOYER

SERVES 8

Soak beans and lentils overnight, rinse and cook in fresh water with the onion "piqué" until soft; reserve beans and liquid separately. On very low heat, sweat chopped onion, garlic, cumin, coriander seed, paprika, saffron and cinnamon in butter for 1 hour. Add ginger and turmeric and sauté for 2 minutes. Add tomatoes and legumes and cook for 30 minutes. Add stock and bean liquor, bring to a boil, and simmer for 35 minutes. Finish with fresh herbs. Remove from heat. Mix lemon juice with eggs and blend into soup. Season with salt and pepper before serving.

Sambhar

GARY HOYER

SERVES 6

1¹/₂ cups / 500 g	carrot/celery root/okra in combination
1	onion, chopped
1 Tbsp. / 15 mL	ground cumin
1 Tbsp. / 15 mL	ground coriander seed
2	dried, red chilies
¹/₂ tsp. / 2.5 mL	black mustard seed
2 Tbsp. / 30 mL	ghee or clarified butter (see page 41)
¹/₂ cup / 120 mL	red lentils, soaked overnight
6 cups / 1.5 L	vegetable stock
¹/₂ tsp. / 2.5 mL	turmeric
2 Tbsp. / 30 mL	ginger
¹/₂	chicken drumstick
¹/₂ cup / 120 mL	yellow dahl
2 Tbsp. / 30 mL	tamarind paste
6	dried curry leaves
¹/₂ tsp. / 2.5 mL	black pepper
pinch	asafoetida
2¹/₂ tsp. / 12.5 mL	salt
4 Tbsp. / 60 mL	fresh coriander
	sea salt and freshly ground black pepper

Sweat vegetables with onion, cumin and coriander seed. Sauté chilies and mustard seed separately in the ghee or clarified butter, and set aside. Add lentils to stock, along with cooked vegetables. Add remaining ingredients, except fresh coriander. Bring to boiling, reduce heat, then simmer for 1 hour. Add the fresh coriander and adjust seasoning.

Gazpacho

GARY HOYER

8	red peppers, seeded, coarsely chopped
8	poblano peppers, seeded, coarsely chopped
2	English cucumbers, coarsely chopped
1/4 cup / 60 mL	shallots
1	small red onion, coarsely chopped
8	cloves garlic
1/2 cup / 120 mL	good sherry vinegar
1 1/2 lbs. / 680 g	fresh ripe tomatoes, coursely chopped
1/2 cup / 120 mL	virgin olive oil
	sea salt and freshly ground black pepper
1 Tbsp / 15 mL	harissa
3 Tbsp. / 45 mL	fresh coriander, chopped
1/2 cup / 120 mL	fresh chives, chopped
1 Tbsp. / 15 mL	fresh parsley, chopped
1 Tbsp. / 15 mL	fresh tarragon, chopped
	juice of 1 lemon
1 1/2 cups / 360 mL	croutons

SERVES 8

In a food processor of blender, and working in batches, coarsely purée all the ingredients except fresh herbs and lemon. Strain through a large-holed sieve or colander. Add herbs, lemon and croutons and adjust seasoning. Chill for at least 2 hours before serving.

Roasted Onion Soup

SIMON KATTAR

This is my version of classic French onion soup. If you like a heartier soup, feel free to add a slice of toasted bread covered with grated Gruyère or crumbled goat cheese. This can be prepared and refrigerated up to 3 days in advance.

SERVES 8

2 Tbsp. / 30 mL	olive oil
1 cup / 240 mL	chopped bacon
2	cloves garlic, chopped
5	whole onions, thinly sliced
8	whole red onions, thinly sliced
4	whole leeks, washed and thinly sliced
4 Tbsp. / 60 mL	rosemary, finely chopped
3	bay leaves
10 cups / 2.4 L	chicken stock

Heat oil in a large stockpot on medium-high heat. Add bacon and cook for about 3 minutes, until the fat begins to melt. Add garlic and cook for another 2 minutes or until lightly roasted.

Add the onions and leeks in several batches, stirring well after each addition. Reduce heat to medium-low, adding 3 Tbsp. (45 mL) of rosemary and bay leaves. Cook for 20–25 minutes, or until onions are well browned and soft.

Increase heat to medium and add chicken stock. Add remaining 1 Tbsp. (15 mL) rosemary and simmer for 30 minutes, or until liquid has reduced by one third. Serve in warmed bowls.

Asparagus Soup

As good as this soup is hot, I also love to serve it chilled. You can substitute broccoli when asparagus is out of season. You can also substitute water to keep this recipe totally vegetarian.

SIMON KATTAR

2 lbs. / 900 g	asparagus, trimmed and peeled
3 Tbsp. / 45 mL	olive oil
2	large onions, thinly sliced
4	cloves garlic, thinly sliced
1	large potato, peeled and chopped
6 cups / 1.5 L	chicken stock
1 Tbsp./ 15 mL	fresh oregano, finely chopped
1	bunch fresh spinach, coarsely chopped
1 cup / 240 mL	feta cheese, crumbled

SERVES 8

First blanch and refresh the asparagus. Bring a large pot of water to a boil and prepare a large bowl with water and ice. Cook asparagus spears until they turn bright green, about 3 minutes. Drain and plunge them into the bowl of ice water to refresh them and seal their colour. Drain, cut off tips and reserve stalks separately.

Heat a large stockpot on medium-low heat and add oil. When hot, add onions and garlic and cook until soft and translucent. Increase heat and add the potato, chicken stock and oregano. Bring to a boil, reduce heat to medium and cook until potatoes are tender, about 20 minutes. Stir in the spinach and cook about 2 minutes longer. Remove from the heat.

Add asparagus stalks. Working in batches, blend in food processor until completely smooth. Strain through a fine-mesh sieve, pressing firmly with the back of a spoon to remove the asparagus fibre and extract as much liquid and flavour as possible.

Return to medium heat and warm soup through, swirl in the feta cheese to enrich the soup. Garnish with asparagus tips and serve.

Root Vegetable and Mushroom Soup

SIMON KATTAR

The wild mushrooms in this soup have an untamed elegance and woody flavour, especially when enhanced with fragrant herbed root vegetables.

SERVES 8

1 oz. / 30 g	dried porcini mushrooms
¼ cup / 60 mL	unsalted butter
1	leek, white part only, sliced
2	cloves garlic, chopped
1	small carrot, peeled and diced
1	small parsnip, peeled and chopped
1	small potato, peeled and diced
6 oz. / 175 g	portobello mushrooms, chopped
6 oz. / 175	oyster mushrooms, chopped
6 oz. / 175 g	shiitake mushrooms, chopped
1 Tbsp. / 15 mL	fresh sage, finely chopped
1 Tbsp. / 15 mL	fresh rosemary, finely chopped
1 Tbsp. / 15 mL	fresh marjoram, finely chopped
1	whole bay leaf
6 cups / 1.5 L	vegetable stock
1 cup / 240 mL	white wine
½ cup / 120 mL	35% cream (optional)
	salt and freshly ground black pepper
	enoki mushrooms, for garnish
1 Tbsp. / 15 mL	chopped fresh parsley, for garnish

Place porcini mushrooms in a small bowl and cover with boiling water. Let soak for about 20 minutes, until tender. Drain mushrooms through a very fine sieve, reserving liquid. If the liquid contains any fine sand, drain through a paper coffee filter.

In a large heavy saucepan, melt butter over medium-high heat. Add leek and garlic and cook until the leek is tender, about 1 minute. Add the carrot, parsnip, potato and porcini mushrooms. Continue to cook until vegetables are tender, about 3 minutes.

Stir in remaining mushrooms and cook for another minute. Add the fresh herbs, bay leaf, vegetable stock, wine and mushroom soaking liquid. Bring to a boil, reduce and simmer until mushrooms are very tender.

Transfer soup to a food processor and process in batches until smooth. Return soup to saucepan and add cream, if using. If soup is too thick, thin with a bit of hot water. Adjust seasoning, adding more salt and pepper as necessary.

To serve, ladle into warm bowls and garnish with enoki mushrooms and chopped parsley.

Pumpkin and Carrot Soup with Mustard

SIMON KATTAR

Use any kind of winter squash or pumpkin in this delightful harvest soup. This soup can be prepared and refrigerated for up to 3 days, or frozen for up to 1 month.

SERVES 6

2 Tbsp. / 30 mL	vegetable oil
3 cups / 720 mL	squash or pumpkin, peeled and cubed
3 cups / 720 mL	carrot, peeled and cubed
1 cup / 240 mL	potato, peeled and cubed
1	large onion, thinly sliced
3 cups / 720 mL	chicken stock
2 Tbsp. / 30 mL	Dijon mustard
	salt and freshly ground black pepper
2 Tbsp. / 30 mL	chopped fresh parsley, for garnish

Heat oil in a large saucepan on low heat and add squash, carrots, potato and onion. Sauté for about 10 minutes. Add stock, cover, and simmer for 40 minutes, stirring occasionally, until vegetables are tender. Add water if needed.

Transfer soup to a food processor or blender and purée in batches until smooth. Transfer to a clean saucepan, add mustard and heat gently until hot. Season with salt and pepper and serve garnished with chopped parsley.

Chilled Pea Soup

For this soup to have the best flavour you should use the very freshest peas. The soup takes only 30 minutes or so to make and it can be kept for a day if stored tightly sealed in the refrigerator.

SIMON KATTAR

1	whole onion
2	whole cloves
6 cups / 1.5 L	chicken stock
1	clove garlic, peeled
2 Tbsp. / 30 mL	fresh tarragon, finely chopped
3 lbs. / 1.35 kg	fresh peas, shelled
3 cups / 720 mL	yogurt
	salt and freshly ground black pepper
2 Tbsp. / 30 mL	fresh mint leaves, for garnish

SERVES 8

Stud the onion with the cloves.

Skewer the onion and the garlic on a wooden skewer.

In a large saucepan, combine chicken stock with the skewer of onion and clove, garlic and tarragon. Bring to a boil, add in the fresh peas and cook for a few minutes until peas are tender.

Discard the onion and garlic skewer. In a blender or food processor blend the soup until smooth. Season with salt and pepper and chill until serving time.

Before serving, mix in the yogurt and adjust the seasoning. Ladle into soup bowls and garnish with mint.

Tomato Consommé

JAMIE KENNEDY

4 lbs. / 2 kg	very ripe tomatoes
3	cloves garlic
1	leek, well washed
1	small celery heart or 2 stalks celery
12	leaves fresh basil or 1 Tbsp. (15 mL) dried
1 tsp. / 5 mL	freshly grated nutmeg
4	egg whites
	salt to taste
10	grinds freshly ground black pepper

MAKES 6 CUPS (1.5 L)

Coarsely chop tomatoes, garlic, leek, celery and basil. Process vegetables approximately 5 seconds in food processor or dice in small pieces. Transfer to a large, heavy-bottomed soup pot. Add nutmeg, egg whites, salt and pepper, and bring quickly to a boil. The egg whites coagulate and form a "raft," capturing the vegetable and clarifying the cosommé. When raft forms, reduce heat and simmer 2 hours. Strain consommé through cheesecloth. Use as required or freeze for later use.

Green Pea Soup with Lettuce

The day that you harvest the first peas from your garden or purchase the first peas from the market is the day to make this soup. Success depends on the sweet freshness of the peas.

JAMIE KENNEDY

For the soup

2 Tbsp. / 30 mL	butter
2	shallots, peeled and cut into brunoise
2 Tbsp. / 30 mL	smoked ham, cut into brunoise
2 cups / 475 mL	fresh green peas
8 cups / 2 L	chicken stock
	salt and freshly ground black pepper

For the garnish

6	leaves of Boston or butter lettuce, washed
3 Tbsp. / 45 mL	blanched fresh green peas
1	basil leaf, cut into julienne

SERVES 6

Melt the butter in a soup pot over low heat. Add the shallot and ham brunoise. Gently sauté for 5 minutes. Add the peas and chicken stock. Cook for 5 minutes or until the peas are tender. Transfer to a blender or food processor and purée. Reserve.

To prepare the garnish, set a vegetable steamer on the stove. Steam the lettuce leaves briefly until they are wilted. Cut the leaves into julienne. Mix with the peas and the basil julienne.

To serve, warm six soup bowls in the oven. Remove them and place an equal amount of garnish in each bowl. Fill each bowl with soup. Grind some black pepper on top. Serve at once.

Chicken and Watercress Soup

JAMIE KENNEDY

This soup has a distinct Asian feel. The combination of chicken, ginger and watercress evokes childhood memories of first-time dining experiences in Chinese restaurants.

For the soup

2 lbs. / 900 g	chicken leg meat, coarsely ground
1	Spanish onion, roughly chopped
1	leek, cleaned and roughly chopped
1	celery root, scrubbed and roughly chopped
1	carrot, peeled and roughly chopped
12	cracked black peppercorns
2	bay leaves
1 Tbsp. / 15 mL	fresh rosemary, roughly chopped
	salt
6	egg whites
12 cups / 3 L	chicken stock

For the garnish

1 Tbsp. / 15 mL	fresh ginger root, peeled and cut into julienne
6	sprigs of watercress
1/2	boneless skinless chicken breast

SERVES 6

Put all the soup ingredients, except the chicken stock, in a large, heavy-bottomed soup pot. Mix thoroughly by hand. Add the stock. Allow the soup to percolate for 2 hours. The ground meat and egg whites will from a raft, clarifying the stock. Pass the liquid through a cheesecloth-lined strainer. Reserve.

Cut the chicken breast into six equal pieces. Pound the pieces as thinly as possible between two sheets of plastic.

To serve, warm six soup bowls. Place some ginger julienne, some watercress leaves, and one slice of pounded chicken breast in each bowl. Ladle boiling consommé over the garnish to cook the chicken. Serve at once.

Clams Steamed in Lovage Broth

Lovage is an herb that tastes like a cross between parsley and celery.
It is a hardy perennial and is one of the first herbs to burst forth in spring.

JAMIE KENNEDY

3 Tbsp. / 45 mL	olive oil
2	cloves garlic, finely chopped
1 Tbsp. / 15 mL	ham, cut into julienne
2	shallots, peeled and cut into brunoise
36	littleneck clams, washed
1 cup / 240 mL	chicken stock
1 cup / 240 mL	dry Riesling wine
2 Tbsp. / 30 mL	lovage leaves, washed and chopped
	salt and freshly ground black pepper

SERVES 6

Heat the olive oil in a large soup pot. Add the garlic, ham and shallots. Sauté gently for 5 minutes. Add the clams. Add the stock and the wine. Bring to the boil and cover. Steam for 5 minutes or until the clams open.

To serve, warm six bowls. Place six clams with their open side facing up in each bowl. Pour the cooking liquid into a blender. With the motor running, add the chopped lovage. Pour the blended broth into each soup bowl and serve at once.

Roasted Vegetable Broth with Arugula Pesto

JAMIE KENNEDY

8 cups / 2 L   Tomato Consommé (see page 52)

For the garnish

3 Tbsp. / 45 mL	sweet potato, finely diced
3 Tbsp. / 45 mL	leek, finely diced
3 Tbsp. / 45 mL	tomato brunoise
3 Tbsp. / 45 mL	zucchini, finely diced

For the arugula pesto

12 leaves	arugula
1	clove garlic, finely chopped
2 Tbsp. / 30 mL	shelled walnuts
6 Tbsp. / 90 mL	fine olive oil
3 Tbsp. / 45 mL	grated Parmigiano-Reggiano cheese
	salt and freshly ground black pepper

SERVES 6

Prepare the Tomato Consommé. Preheat an oven to 350°F (175°C). Place all the vegetables, except the tomato, in a cast iron frying pan. Place the pan in the oven and roast, stirring from time to time, until the vegetables have shrivelled slightly and browned somewhat. Remove from the oven and reserve.

Roughly chop the arugula leaves and place them in a blender. Add the garlic and walnuts. Turn the blender on and, with the motor running, add the olive oil in a steady stream. Add the grated Parmigiano-Reggiano. Transfer to a bowl and season with salt and pepper.

To serve, heat soup to simmering point. Place some roasted vegetables and some tomato brunoise in each bowl. Place a dollop of pesto on top. Ladle hot soup into each bowl. Serve at once.

Clams Steamed in Lovage Broth   p. 55

BOWL BY PAULA MURRAY

Jerusalem Artichoke with
White Truffle Oil   p. 80

Baked Tomato Water with Black Truffle
and Lemongrass   p. 69

BOWL BY THOMAS AITKEN

Roasted Red Pepper Soup with
Semolina Dumplings   p. 57

BOWL BY SARAH RAYMOND

Roasted Red Pepper Soup with Semolina Dumplings

JAMIE KENNEDY

For the soup

1 Tbsp. / 15 mL	olive oil for cooking
3	cloves garlic, finely chopped
1 Tbsp. / 15 mL	fresh oregano leaves
1 quart jar / 1 L jar	roasted red peppers
8 cups / 2 L	Tomato Consommé (see page 52)
	salt and freshly ground black pepper

For the dumplings

1 cup / 240 mL	milk
2	eggs
3 Tbsp. / 45 mL	melted butter
$1/3$ cup / 80 mL	semolina flour
$1/3$ cup / 80 mL	all-purpose flour
3 Tbsp. / 45 mL	parsley, roughly chopped
$1/4$ tsp. / 1.2 mL	ground nutmeg
	salt to taste

SERVES 6

Add olive oil and garlic into a large soup pot over medium heat. Sauté briefly, but don't let garlic brown. Add the red peppers and oregano and continue to sauté for 5 minutes. Add the consommé and simmer for 30 minutes. Purée the soup, then heat it to a simmer. Adjust seasoning with salt and pepper.

Pour the milk and eggs into a stainless steel bowl and let them come to room temperature. Mix in the melted butter, semolina and flour. Add the parsley, nutmeg and salt to taste. Mix well. Boil a large saucepan of salted water.

Let the dough rest for 30 minutes, then form small round dumplings with a teaspoon—you should have 18 dumplings—and drop them into the water. Simmer the dumplings for 10 minutes. Test for doneness by slicing one in half to see if it is cooked all the way through. Keep the dumplings warm in the cooking water.

To serve, place three dumplings in each of six warmed soup bowls. Ladle soup over them. Serve at once.

Black Bean and Chipotle Soup with Lime

MARTIN KOUPRIE

SERVES 8

For the soup

2 Tbsp. / 30 mL	unsalted butter
1/2 cup / 120 mL	celery, chopped
1/2 cup / 120 mL	Spanish onion, chopped
2 Tbsp. / 30 mL	double-smoked bacon, diced
1 tsp. / 5 mL	ground cumin
1 tsp. / 5 mL	coriander seed
1 Tbsp. / 15 mL	chipotle peppers
1	bay leaf
1 Tbsp. / 15 mL	fresh garlic, chopped
2 lbs. / 900 g	dried black beans, soaked overnight
12–14 cups / 3–3.5 L	homemade chicken stock (see page 63)
2	limes, juice and zest
	sea salt
1 tsp. / 5 mL	red wine vinegar

In a large pan over medium-high heat, cook the butter, celery, onions and bacon until vegetables are tender. Add the cumin, coriander seed, chipotle peppers, bay leaf and garlic. Add drained beans and 12 cups (3 L) chicken stock and cook until tender. keep remainder of chicken stock hot in separate pot.

Add the lime zest, lime juice and red wine vinegar and lightly season with salt.

Working in small batches, purée the soup in a blender until smooth. Pass the purée through a coarse strainer and adjust with more boiling chicken stock if too thick. Taste and adjust seasoning if necessary. It may be necessary to add more vinegar to balance the soup.

For the garnish

1 cup / 240 mL	sour cream
1 cup / 240 mL	tomato, peeled and diced
1 tsp. / 5 mL	lime zest

To serve, warm the bowls in the oven. Spoon out even portions and garnish with sour cream topped with diced tomato and lime zest.

Butternut Squash and Apple Soup with Maple-Bourbon Foam

MARTIN KOUPRIE

3 Tbsp. / 45 mL	unsalted butter
1/2 cup / 120 mL	Spanish onion, chopped
3 lbs. / 1.35 kg	butternut squash, chopped
3/4 lb. / 340 g	tart apples, peeled, seeded and chopped
9–10 cups / 2.2–2.5 L	chicken stock
1 Tbsp. / 15 mL	sea salt
3 tsp. / 15 mL	red wine vinegar (or to taste)
2 cups / 475 mL	35% cream
1 Tbsp. / 15 mL	dark maple syrup
1 Tbsp. / 15 mL	bourbon
1 tsp. / 5 mL	vanilla extract
6	sprigs fresh coriander

SERVES 6

In a large pan over medium-high heat, heat the butter and onions. Cook until tender. Add the squash and apples and cook until they have completely broken down to a pulp. Before you begin adding liquid, allow the ingredients to caramelize on the bottom of the pot. As they begin to do so, use a wooden spoon to scrape the bottom and prevent the glazed squash and apple from burning. Add some stock when necessary. When the ingredients are darkened enough, add the 9 cups (2.2 L) stock and bring to a boil. Season lightly with salt.

In a blender, working in small batches, purée the soup until smooth. Pass the purée through a coarse strainer and thin with more boiling chicken stock if necessary. Taste and adjust seasoning to taste. Add just a touch of red wine vinegar to the soup to help bring up the acidity to better reveal the apple flavours. You should add only enough to enhance the apples—you should *not* be able to taste the vinegar!

In a cold stainless steel bowl, whip together the cream, maple syrup, bourbon and vanilla extract to stiff peaks. This may take a little longer than usual because of the extra liquid that the cream has to carry. An electric mixer will facilitate the process for you.

To serve, warm the soup bowls in the oven. Spoon out even portions and garnish with the maple foam in the middle of each bowl. Serve with a sprig of coriander placed standing up in the foam.

Shellfish Bisque

MARTIN KOUPRIE

For the bisque

1¹/₂ lbs. / 680 g	raw lobster or shrimp shells
2 Tbsp. / 30 mL	unsalted butter
1	onion, chopped
2	carrot, chopped
2	stalks celery, chopped
¹/₂ cup / 120 mL	brandy
1	5.5-oz. can (156-g) tomato paste
¹/₂ cup / 120 mL	all-purpose flour
4 cups / 950 mL	fish stock
4 cups / 950 mL	chicken stock
1 tsp. / 5 mL	caraway seed
1	bay leaf
¹/₂ cup / 120 mL	35% cream
1 tsp. / 5 mL	vanilla extract
	salt and freshly ground black pepper

SERVES 6

TIP
Instead of buying whole lobsters, crabs or shrimp, ask your fishmonger or a local restaurant to save shells for you. Most vendors will provide shells free of charge to regular customers.

Pulse shells in food processor until coarsely chopped. (Alternatively, wrap the shells in an old tea towel and twist the ends together to form a bundle. Using a mallet, smash the shells to a pulp.)

Melt the butter in a large saucepan. Add the onion, carrots and celery; cook on medium-low heat for about 10 minutes or until very soft.

Add the crushed shells and continue cooking, stirring frequently, for 3 minutes or until colour changes. Do not scorch! Increase heat to medium. Deglaze with brandy—bring to boil. Stir in tomato paste and cook, stirring often, for 5 minutes. Stirring constantly, dust the mixture with flour, adding a little stock if mixture begins to scorch. Cook, stirring for 5 minutes; gradually add fish and chicken stocks, caraway seed and bay leaf.

Bring mixture to boil. Reduce heat to low and simmer for 45 minutes. Discard bay leaf and purée bisque in blender. Strain and return bisque to the stove; bring to a boil. Whisk in cream and vanilla and simmer for 3 minutes. Season with salt and pepper to taste.

For the garnish

1 tsp. / 5 mL	unsalted butter
1	clove garlic, minced
1/2 cup / 120 mL	fresh corn kernels
8	large shrimp or scallops, cleaned
1/4 tsp. / 1.2 mL	salt
1/4 tsp. / 1.2 mL	pepper

Heat butter in skillet set over medium heat; add garlic and cook, stirring occasionally, for 30 seconds. Increase heat to medium-high and add corn; cook, stirring often for 2 minutes or until browned. Add shrimp or scallops and sauté for 1 minute or until almost opaque; season with salt and pepper.

Place a shrimp or scallop and some corn in bottom of each bowl; ladle hot bisque over top. Serve immediately.

Corn and Fennel Purée With Chanterelles

MARTIN KOUPRIE

This bright yellow soup, punctuated with chanterelles, has the consistency of a cream soup without any cream! It is low in fat and high in fibre since most of the calories are derived from vegetables.

For the soup

SERVES 4

2 Tbsp. / 30 mL	unsalted butter
1/2 cup / 120 mL	Spanish onion, diced
4 cups / 950 mL	fresh corn kernels
1 cup / 240 mL	fennel bulb, diced
2	cloves garlic, minced
1 tsp. / 5 mL	sea salt
6 cups / 1.5 L	chicken stock (see page 63)

In a pot over medium-high heat, add the butter and onion and cook until tender. Add the corn, fennel and garlic and cook for 10 minutes or until they are steaming in the pot and hot to touch! Add the chicken stock and bring to a boil; reduce temperature to a simmer, and cook for 20 minutes. Season lightly with salt.

In a blender, in small batches, purée the soup until smooth. Pass the purée through a coarse strainer to remove any of the corn pulp and adjust the consistency with boiling chicken stock if too thick. Taste and adjust seasonings.

For the garnish:

1 Tbsp. / 15 mL	unsalted butter
1 tsp. / 5 mL	shallot, minced
1/4 lb. / 113 g	medium chanterelles
1/2 tsp. / 2.5 mL	garlic, minced
1/3 cup / 80 mL	white wine
1/4 tsp. / 1.2 mL	lemon juice
pinch	sea salt
pinch	freshly ground black pepper

In a pan over medium-high heat, add the butter with the shallots and sauté until tender. Add the chanterelles and sauté until tender. Add minced garlic and deglaze with white wine. Reduce the wine by two-thirds, add a few drops of lemon juice (no more than that) and season with salt and pepper.

To serve, warm the bowls in the oven. Ladle soup into bowls and place the hot chanterelles on top.

Optional

Although store-bought chicken stock preparations are low in fat, they can be very high in sodium. So, if you like to cook with stock or if you make soup often, you may want to try making your own chicken stock. All you need is a large pot and a few inexpensive ingredients: throw into the pot $1/2$ lb. (225 g) chicken bones (most butchers will give them to you or sell them inexpensively), a tomato, some chopped onion, a carrot and two or three stalks of celery, a bay leaf and enough cold water to just cover it all. Bring the mixture to a boil and reduce heat to low; simmer for 4 hours and strain through a fine mesh sieve. Place stock in refrigerator until very cold; scrape off any congealed fat and discard. Season lightly with salt and pepper. Voilà!

Parsnip and Lemon Soup

MARTIN KOUPRIE

2 Tbsp. / 30 mL	unsalted butter
2 cups / 475 mL	Spanish onion, peeled and diced
2 lbs. / 900 g	parsnip, peeled and diced
12 cups / 3 L	homemade chicken stock (see page 63)
4	lemons, zest
	salt
1 cup / 240 mL	35% cream, whipped
1 Tbsp. / 15 mL	fresh tarragon

SERVES 8

In a large pan over medium heat, melt the butter, add the onion and sauté until tender. Add the parsnip and cook until pulpy. Add a little chicken stock at times to avoid scorching the bottom of the pot. Add the lemon zest and all but 1 cup (240 mL) of the stock and bring to a boil. After 5 minutes, remove from heat and season lightly.

In a blender, purée the soup in batches and adjust with a little chicken stock to thin. Taste and adjust seasoning.

To serve, warm the bowls in the oven. Fold the whipped cream and tarragon. Spoon even portions of soup into each bowl and garnish with cream mixture.

Ontario Plum Soup with White Chocolate and Grappa Sorbet

SUSUR LEE

15	ripe plums, pits removed and chopped
1¹/₂ cups / 375 mL	Alsatian white wine
1 Tbsp. / 15 mL	wildflower honey
1 recipe	White Chocolate and Grappa Sorbet (see below)

Bring plums, wine and honey to a boil. Remove from heat. Purée and strain with a fine strainer; cool in the fridge.

White Chocolate and Grappa Sorbet

SERVES 4

1 cup / 240 mL	white chocolate, chopped
3 cups / 720 mL	water
¹/₂ cup / 120 mL	sugar
¹/₂ tsp. / 2.5 mL	lemon zest

Put water, sugar and chocolate in a double boiler until melted. Remove. Add zest and cool. Place in an ice cream machine and churn until frozen, according to manufacturer's directions.

Ladle soup into a bowl and place a scoop of sorbet in the centre, garnish and serve.

Egg Drop Soup with Dungeness Crab Square

SUSUR LEE

For the spatzle dough

1¹/₂ cups / 360 mL	milk
2 cups / 475 mL	all-purpose flour
4	whole eggs
	salt and freshly ground black pepper

Bring salted water to a boil, push dough through a screen to form little balls, add to boiling water; when dough floats it is cooked—about 5 minutes—and should be strained.

SERVES 2

For the crab square

2 Tbsp. / 30 mL	puréed potato
1 cup / 240 mL	fresh crab meat
1 Tbsp. / 15 mL	fresh chives, chopped
¹/₂ Tbsp. / 7.5 mL	egg white
	salt and freshly ground black pepper

Mix ingredients together to form a sticky paste. To cook squares: Using a square cookie cutter, push crab mixture into the bottom and fill the top with the cooked spatzle. Remove from mould and pan-fry until golden brown or roast in the oven for 10 minutes at 350°F (175°C).

For the soup

2 cups / 475 mL	white chicken stock
2	eggs, beaten
¹/₄ cup / 60 mL	Parmesan cheese, grated
4	sprigs Italian parsley

Heat stock to boiling, reduce heat and whisk in eggs. Remove from heat and add cheese.

To serve, reheat soup, place a crab square in each bowl, ladle soup over top and garnish with parsley sprigs.

Chilled Apple Curry Soup with Beet Relish

SUSUR LEE

2 Tbsp. / 30 mL	vegetable oil
1	medium Spanish onion, chopped
2	apples
1/2 cup / 120 mL	celery, diced
1/2 cup / 120 mL	carrots, sliced
4	cloves garlic, chopped
2 tsp. / 10 mL	fresh ginger, finely chopped
2 Tbsp. / 30 mL	fresh cilantro leaves, chopped
1 1/2 Tbsp./ 22.5 mL	West Indian curry powder
1	medium potato, chopped
10 cups / 2.4 L	chicken stock
	salt
1 cup / 240 mL	10% cream
1 recipe	Beet Relish (see below)

SERVES 6

Heat oil in Dutch oven and add the onion, apples, celery, carrots, garlic, ginger, cilantro, curry powder and potato. Sauté together until soft. Transfer to soup pot. Add chicken stock and salt and cook for 1/2 hour. Purée and cool in refrigerator. When cool add cream. Garnish with beet relish and freshly chopped mint leaves.

Beet Relish

2 Tbsp. / 30 mL	vegetable oil
1	beet, diced
1	onion, diced
1	apple, diced
1 tsp. / 5 mL	red wine vinegar
1/2 tsp. / 2.5 mL	honey
	salt
1/2 cup / 120 mL	red wine

Heat vegetable oil in a frying pan and sauté beet, onion, apple and vinegar together until soft. Add honey, salt and wine and cook with lid on for 20 minutes. Cool.

Hot and Sour Egg Drop Soup with Quail

SUSUR LEE

SERVES 4

3	quails, boned
1	recipe Chinese Marinade (see next page)
	peanut oil, for deep-frying
6 cups / 1.5 L	chicken stock
2	shallots, cut in fine half moons
1 tsp. / 5 mL	fresh ginger, finely julienned
1 cup / 240 mL	black tree ear mushrooms (or wild), finely sliced
1/2 cup / 120 mL	shiitake mushrooms, finely sliced and stems removed
1/2	roasted red pepper, julienned
1/2 cup / 120 mL	tomato, chopped
pinch	white pepper
1 1/2 Tbsp. / 22.5 mL	freshly grated Parmesan cheese (preferably Reggiano)
2	whole eggs
1 tsp. / 5 mL	sesame oil
2	hot Thai red chilies
1 tsp. / 5 mL	sugar
	chopped chives, for garnish
	chopped coriander, for garnish
	balsamic vinegar (good quality, wood-aged)

Marinate quail in Chinese Marinade for 2 days. Remove from marinade, scrape and pat dry. Heat oil over medium heat and deep-fry for 8 minutes or until outside is brown and crispy. Remove from oil, drain and set aside.

Combine all ingredients except Parmesan cheese, eggs, sesame oil and garnish, in a heavy bottom pot. Bring to a boil, cover and simmer for 8–10 minutes. Whip together Parmesan cheese and egg. Bring soup back to a boil and drop egg mixture into soup. Stir gently. Garnish with sesame oil, herbs and vinegar and serve immediately.

Chinese Marinade

1/2 cup / 120 mL	maple syrup
1	stalk celery, diced
1	medium carrot, diced
1	medium Spanish onion, diced
1 Tbsp. / 15 mL	minced fresh ginger
1 Tbsp. / 15 mL	minced mint
1/4 cup /60 mL	coriander, minced
1 tsp. / 5 mL	black peppercorns
1 Tbsp. / 15 mL	sherry or Marsala
1 Tbsp. / 15 mL	sesame oil
1/4 cup /60 mL	soy sauce

Combine all ingredients in a non-reactive bowl, add the quail and marinate for two days.

Baked Tomato Water with Black Truffle and Lemongrass

20	medium very ripe field tomatoes
	kosher salt and freshly ground black pepper
1	bay leaf
1	stalk lemongrass, chopped (discard hard parts)
8	slices fresh black or white truffles

Bake tomatoes in a heavy-bottomed roasting pan for 90 minutes at 275°F (135°C). Remove skin from tomato, purée and place mixture in a cheese-cloth. Hang up overnight with a pot underneath to collect all the water.

Place collected liquid in a pot with salt, pepper and bay leaf and bring to a boil. Remove from heat. Remove bay leaf, add truffles and lemongrass. Serve.

Celery Root and Foie Gras Soup with Jerusalem Artichoke Chips

MARGARET MACKAY

2	leeks, white part only, chopped
1 Tbsp. / 15 mL	chopped garlic
2 Tbsp. / 30 mL	unsalted butter
5 cups / 1.2 L	chicken stock
8	large heads celery root, peeled and diced
1/4 lb. / 113 g	foie gras, deveined
	sea salt
	Jerusalem artichokes (Sunchokes), well scrubbed, thinly shaved and deep-fried, for garnish
	finely chopped chives, for garnish

SERVES 4

Sweat leeks and garlic in butter until soft, but not browned. Add chicken stock and celery root. Simmer until celery root is very soft. Purée, while still hot, until very smooth with the foie gras. Season with sea salt.

Soup should be handblended just before serving as foie gras fat will separate.

Garnish with Jerusalem artichokes and chopped chives before serving.

Potato-Leek and 4-Year-Old Ontario Cheddar Soup

MARGARET MACKAY

2	leeks, chopped
1	onion, chopped
1/4 cup / 60 mL	bacon fat
4	medium Yukon Gold potatoes, chopped
6 cups. / 1.5 L	chicken stock
2 Tbsp. / 30 mL	fresh thyme, chopped
1 1/2 cups / 360 mL	4-year-old Ontario cheddar cheese, grated

Using a Dutch oven, cook the leeks and onions on medium-low heat in the bacon fat. Do not allow them to brown. Add chopped potatoes, chicken stock and thyme. Cook until potatoes are tender, about 20 minutes and stir in cheddar. Serve at once.

SERVES 4

Scallop Soup with Organic Vegetables

MARGARET MACKAY

1 cup / 240 mL	dry white Canadian wine
1 cup / 240 mL	fish stock
1/2 cup / 120 mL	organic red and yellow carrot, julienned
1/2 cup / 120 mL	organic red turnip, julienned
1/2 cup / 120 mL	organic leek (tender whites and green), julienned
12	pink swimming sea scallops, or bay scallops
	sea salt and freshly ground black pepper

SERVES 2

In a medium saucepan, bring wine, stock, carrot and turnip to a boil. Reduce heat and simmer for 5 minutes until vegetables are tender-crisp. Meanwhile steam leeks in a vegetable steamer. Set aside.

Place 6 scallops and leek julienne in hot bowls. Ladle piping hot broth over scallops. Season with salt and pepper.

Roasted Tomato Soup with Sweet Corn and Pumpkin

MARGARET MACKAY

12	very ripe field tomatoes
2 tsp. / 10 mL	fresh garlic, chopped
2 tsp. / 10 mL	shallot, chopped
2	leeks, white part only, chopped
1 Tbsp. / 15 mL	canola oil
16 cups / 4 L	chicken stock
	sea salt and freshly ground black pepper

For the garnish

1	cob sweet corn, kernels removed
2 Tbsp. / 30 mL	pumpkin, diced
1 tsp. / 5 mL	organic canola oil
	salt
	fresh whole coriander seeds

MAKES 24 CUPS (6 L)

Slice and spread the tomatoes on cookie sheets in a single layer. Bake at 225°F (105°C) for approximately 3½ hours until dried out but not browned.

Sweat garlic, shallot and leeks in canola oil. Add tomatoes and chicken stock. Simmer for 20 minutes. Pass through a medium-gauge strainer to remove seeds. Season with salt and pepper.

Preheat oven to 350°F (175°C). To prepare the garnish, mix together the corn kernels and diced pumpkin. Toss with canola oil and salt. Roast, covered, until pumpkin is cooked through, about 20 minutes.

To serve, spoon 2 Tbsp. (30 mL) of garnish in a tall mound in the centre of each heated soup bowl. Ladle in hot soup. Rub fresh coriander seeds lightly (to release fragrant oils), sprinkle over the soup and serve immediately.

Wild Ginger and Young Spinach Soup

MARGARET MACKAY

2 oz. / 50 g	wild ginger
1	leek, white part only, chopped
2 Tbsp. / 30 mL	garlic, chopped
2 Tbsp. / 30 mL	butter
8 cups / 2 L	chicken stock
2 lbs. / 900 g	Yukon Gold potatoes, roughly chopped
	salt and freshly ground black pepper
2	bunches spinach
2	sprigs thyme
2 Tbsp. / 15 mL	Italian parsley, chopped
	finely chopped chives, for garnish

SERVES 6

In a hot soup pot, sauté ginger, leek and garlic in butter. Add chicken stock and potatoes, lightly season, and cook until potatoes are tender, about 20 minutes. Add spinach and cook for 1 minute (must be bright green). Remove from heat.

Purée soup and strain. Adjust seasoning.

Garnish with chives before serving.

Crab Chilpachole

CHRISTOPHER MCDONALD

1	large Dungeness crab (about 2 lbs./900 g)
1/2	large onion, thickly sliced
6	cloves garlic, peeled
5	medium tomatoes (about 1 1/2 lbs./680 g)
2	chipotle chilies
1	ancho chili, lightly roasted, soaked, seeded and deveined
1 Tbsp. / 15 mL	tomato paste
3 Tbsp. / 45 mL	olive oil
	salt
6	sprigs fresh epazote
	cilantro sprigs, for garnish
	lime juice, to taste

SERVES 5

In a large saucepan, bring 1 1/2 qts. (1.5 L) of lightly salted water to a boil. Scrub the crab well under cold water and drop into boiling water. Cook for 15 minutes. Remove crab and let it cool. Keep water at a simmer.

When the crab is cool enough to handle, work over a bowl to first remove the heart-shaped piece of shell on the front. Then pry off the back shell. Scrape the white fat and little orange eggs, if any, from the shell and the crab itself. Using a mortar and pestle, grind together to a paste, adding the liquid from the bowl and any tomalley. Remove the small spongy gills and discard. Pick meat from the shell and claws. Set meat aside.

Break up the shells and let them simmer in the cooking water (add more water if they are not completely covered) for at least 60 minutes. Strain the resulting broth through cheesecloth and set aside.

Preheat a griddle or cast-iron pan. Wrap the onion slices and garlic together in foil; wrap the tomatoes separately in parchment paper. Roast both packages on the griddle or pan until they are cooked through, about 20 minutes. Place contents of foil packages in a blender with 1/2 cup (120 mL) of reserved broth, chipotle and ancho chilies, and the tomato paste. Purée until smooth.

(continued on next page)

Heat the olive oil in a deep saucepan and cook the purée for about 10 minutes over high heat, stirring occasionally. Add the rest of the crab broth and the epazote to the tomato sauce and let it simmer for about 5 minutes. Add salt as necessary. Remove the epazote. Whisk in paste to thicken the soup slightly. Let the soup simmer for a moment longer; do not boil. Adjust to taste with salt and lime juice.

Divide reserved crab meat evenly among soup bowls. Ladle broth over crab and serve garnished with sprigs of cilantro.

Fresh Corn Chowder with Roasted Red Pepper Cream

CHRISTOPHER MCDONALD

3	cobs fresh sweet corn
2 Tbsp. / 30 mL	unsalted butter
1/2	medium onion, finely chopped
2	cloves garlic, peeled and minced
2 cups / 480 mL	milk, plus a little more if necessary
1	baking potato, peeled and diced into 1/4-inch (.6-cm) cubes
1	bay leaf
1	poblano chili, roasted and peeled, seeded and finely diced
1 cup / 240 mL	35% cream
1 tsp. / 5 mL	salt
1 recipe	Roasted Red Pepper Cream (see below)

SERVES 4

Husk and remove all corn silk from the ears of corn, then cut the kernels from each cob with a sharp knife. There should be 2 1/2–3 cups (600–720 mL) of corn.

Heat the butter in a soup pot over medium heat. Add the onion and fry until soft, 6–7 minutes, then stir in the garlic and cook for a minute longer.

Add the milk, corn, potato and bay leaf; partially cover and simmer for 15 minutes over medium-low heat, stirring often.

When the potato is tender, stir in the chili and whipping cream. Season with salt and simmer over medium-low heat for 10 minutes longer, stirring frequently. Serve in heated soup bowls garnished with Roasted Red Pepper Cream.

Roasted Red Pepper Cream

1/2 cup / 120 mL	35% cream, whipped
1	red pepper, roasted, peeled and puréed
	salt
1/2 tsp. / 2.5 mL	lemon juice

Combine all ingredients.

Avalon's Cauliflower and Clam "Chowder" with Caviar and Crème Fraîche

CHRISTOPHER MCDONALD

SERVES 6

2 lbs. / 900 g	clams (littleneck, if available)
3 cups / 720 mL	chicken stock
2 Tbsp. / 30 mL	unsalted butter
1	leek, finely chopped
1	medium cauliflower, broken into flowerettes, with stems roughly chopped
	juice of $1/2$ lemon
dash	hot pepper sauce
4 Tbsp. / 60 mL	unsalted butter, chilled
$1/2$ cup / 120 mL	35% cream, lightly whipped
	salt and freshly ground white pepper

For the garnish

6	large root vegetable chips, or good-quality potato chips, lightly salted
1 cup / 240 mL	crème fraîche or good-quality sour cream, mixed with 2 Tbsp. (30 mL) finely chopped chives
1 oz. / 30 g	Sevruga caviar

Steam clams in 1 cup (240 mL) of the chicken stock until opened, about 4 minutes. Remove clams from heat and let cool. Remove clams from shell and set aside; discard shells. Strain the stock through cheesecloth or a coffee filter to remove any sand and reserve with additional stock.

Melt 2 Tbsp. (30 mL) butter in a large pot and gently sauté leeks until soft but not browned, about 5 minutes. Add cauliflower. Pour in chicken stock, including the cup (240 mL) used for the clams. Bring to a simmer and continue simmering, uncovered, for 5 minutes. Remove 6 of the largest flowerettes and set aside. Continue to simmer the rest of the cauliflower until it is very tender, about 5 more minutes.

Purée cauliflower, leeks and stock together in a food processor or blender; pass through a sieve back into the pot, pressing mixture with the back of a spoon to extract as much liquid as possible. Discard what is left in the sieve. Return the pot to heat and bring to a simmer. Add clams. Remove from heat and add salt and pepper to taste. Add lemon juice and hot pepper sauce. Whisk in 4 Tbsp. (60 mL) butter and fold in whipped cream.

Have ready 6 heated bowls. Place a cauliflower flowerette in the bottom of each bowl and ladle soup over top. On top of each flowerette, place a vegetable or potato chip topped with a dollop of the chive crème fraîche and 1 Tbsp. (15 mL) caviar. Serve immediately.

Jerusalem Artichoke Soup with White Truffle Oil

CHRISTOPHER MCDONALD

2 lbs. / 900 g	Jerusalem artichokes, peeled
2 Tbsp. / 30 mL	unsalted butter
1/2 lb. / 225 g	celery root, peeled and finely sliced
2	large onions, finely chopped
6 cups / 1.5 L	chicken stock
	salt and white pepper
	lemon juice to taste
1 cup / 240 mL	35% cream, whipped
	chopped fresh Italian parsley, for garnish
	white truffle oil (optional), for garnish

SERVES 6

Finely slice artichokes and place in a bowl of cold water to prevent blackening. In a large saucepan, melt butter over medium heat. Gently sauté the celery root and onions until soft. Drain artichokes and add to saucepan with chicken stock. Simmer for 20 minutes until tender. Remove from heat; allow to cool slightly and transfer to a blender. Working in batches, purée until smooth and pass through a fine sieve. Return soup to saucepan, reheat over medium heat, and season with salt, pepper and a few drops of lemon juice to taste. Just before serving, stir in the whipped cream.

Serve in wide preheated soup bowls garnished with parsley and a drizzle of truffle oil if using.

Soupe au Pistou   p. 98

Carrot and Turnip Soup   p. 86

BOWL BY CAROLYNN BLOOMER

Corn and Fennel Purée
with Chanterelles   p. 62

BOWL BY MARNI LOCKINGTON

Cold Summer Friut Soup
with Vanilla Anglaise   p. 103

BOWL BY MARNI LOCKINGTON

Baked Pepper and Onion Soup with Asiago Croutons

2 Tbsp. / 30 mL	unsalted butter
5 cups / 1.2 L	red and green peppers, sliced
5 cups / 1.2 L	Spanish onions, sliced
1 Tbsp. / 15 mL	garlic, finely chopped
	salt and freshly ground black pepper
2 Tbsp. / 30 mL	tomato paste
6 cups / 1.5 L	beef stock
1 Tbsp. / 15 mL	fresh rosemary, chopped
1 Tbsp. / 15 mL	fresh oregano, chopped
1/4 cup / 60 mL	fresh basil chiffonade (see page 14)
1	baguette
1/2 cup / 120 mL	Asiago, thinly sliced
	fresh herb sprigs, for garnish

SERVES 12

In a soup pot, melt butter and sauté peppers, onions and garlic until onions are translucent.

Add salt, pepper and tomato paste and cook for 1 minute over medium heat. Add beef stock and bring to a boil. Reduce heat, add rosemary, oregano and basil, and simmer for 20 minutes.

Ladle soup portions into bowls and place bowls in a baking dish. Cover each soup with a toasted slice of baguette topped with thin slices of Asiago. Bake in the oven at 375°F (190°C) for 15 minutes. Garnish with herb sprigs.

great soup empty bowls 81

Sugar Snap Pea Soup with Stilton

KENNETH PEACE

3 Tbsp. / 45 mL	unsalted butter
1 cup / 240 mL	onion, chopped
1 cup / 240 mL	leeks, chopped
1 cup / 240 mL	celery, chopped
3 Tbsp. / 45 mL	all-purpose flour
6 cups / 1.5 L	chicken stock
4 cups / 950 mL	sugar snap peas
1 Tbsp. / 15 mL	fresh mint, chopped
3/4 cup / 180 mL	10% cream
	salt and freshly ground black pepper
1/2 cup / 120 mL	crumbled Stilton
	fresh mint sprigs, for garnish

SERVES 12

Melt butter and sauté onion, leek and celery until onion is translucent. Dust mixture with flour and stir to form a roux. Add chicken stock, mix well and bring to a boil over medium heat.

Remove from heat, stir in peas, mint and cream and let stand for 15 minutes.

Purée soup in food processor, add salt and pepper. Serve reheated and topped with some crumbled Stilton. Garnish with sprig of mint.

Corn Chowder with Seared Pimentone Shrimp

KENNETH PEACE

3 Tbsp. / 45 mL	unsalted butter
1 cup / 240 mL	onion, diced
1 cup / 240 mL	celery, diced
2 cups / 475 mL	potatoes, diced
1/2 cup / 120 mL	carrots, diced
1/2 cup / 120 mL	red pepper, diced
1/2 tsp. / 2.5 mL	saffron
6 cups / 1.5 L	fresh corn kernels
3 Tbsp. / 45 mL	all-purpose flour
8 cups / 2 L	chicken stock
	salt and freshly ground black pepper
1/2 cup / 120 mL	10% cream
4 Tbsp. / 60 mL	fresh cilantro, finely chopped
1 1/2 lbs. / 680 g	tiger shrimp, shelled and cut in half lengthwise
2 Tbsp. / 30 mL	olive oil
1 Tbsp. / 15 mL	pimentone or smoked paprika
	salt and freshly ground black pepper

SERVES 12

Melt butter and sauté onion, celery, potatoes, carrots and peppers until onion is translucent. Add saffron and corn and cook for 1 minute. Dust mixture with flour and stir to form a roux. Add chicken stock, mix well and bring to a boil over medium heat.

Reduce heat, add salt and pepper, cream and cilantro and simmer for 20 minutes.

Meanwhile, marinate shrimp in a mixture of olive oil, pimentone or smoked paprika, salt and pepper. Sauté shrimp over high heat, just until cooked. Garnish each bowl of soup with some shrimp and serve at once.

Roasted Duck and Mushroom Soup with Celery Root Crisps

KENNETH PEACE

SERVES 12

3 Tbsp. / 45 mL	unsalted butter
1 cup / 240 mL	onion, diced
1 cup / 240 mL	celery, diced
1 lb. / 455 g	mushrooms (crimini, portobello, shiitake), sliced
3 Tbsp. / 45 mL	all-purpose flour
8 cups / 2 L	chicken stock
3 cups / 720 mL	cooked duck meat, julienned (from one 3–4 lb./1.35–1.8 kg roasted duck)
	vegetable oil
1 cup / 240 mL	celery root, julienned
	salt

Melt butter and sauté onion, celery and mushrooms until mushrooms brown slightly. Dust mixture with flour and stir to form a roux. Add chicken stock, mix well and bring to a boil over medium heat.

Reduce heat, add duck meat and simmer for 1 hour.

Meanwhile, julienne the celery root, deep-fry in vegetable oil, drain and add salt to taste. Use to garnish soup.

Lobster and Asparagus Consommé with Tarragon

KENNETH PEACE

3 lbs. / 1.35 kg	lobsters, blanched
2 cups / 475 mL	onion, finely chopped
2 cups / 475 mL	celery, finely chopped
5 cups / 1.2 L	tomatoes, finely chopped
1 Tbsp. / 15 mL	black peppercorns
1 Tbsp. / 15 mL	salt
8	egg whites
3 cups / 720 mL	asparagus, finely chopped
1 cup / 240 mL	fresh tarragon, chopped
8 cups / 2 L	cold water
	tarragon sprigs, for garnish

SERVES 12

Remove meat from blanched lobsters and set aside. Roast the lobster shells until dark red.

Crush lobster shells, mix with onion, celery, tomatoes, peppercorns, salt, egg whites, asparagus—set aside tips and tarragon. Mix together well and allow to stand refrigerated for 1 hour.

Place mixture in a large pot, add the water and bring to a boil until "raft" forms on top of consommé. Reduce heat and simmer for 2 hours. Remove raft and strain consommé through cheesecloth.

Meanwhile, blanch asparagus tips

Garnish soup with lobster meat, asparagus tips and tarragon leaves.

Carrot and Turnip Soup

YASSER QAHAWISH

1 lb. / 455 g   carrots, peeled and washed
1/2 lb. / 225 g   white turnip, peeled and washed
3 1/2 oz. / 100 g   unsalted butter
8 cups / 2 L   cold chicken stock or cold water
salt and fresh ground black pepper
fresh chervil, for garnish
crème fraîche, for garnish

Vegetarian option: instead of chicken stock, substitute 1 medium onion and 8 cups (2 L) water or vegetable stock.

SERVES 6

Grate carrots and turnip (and onion, if using) in a food processor with grater attachment or by hand.

Melt butter in soup pot, add grated vegetables, cover, and cook over low heat for 5 minutes.

Add cold chicken or vegetable stock or water. Cook over high heat and bring to a boil.

Season with salt and pepper and reduce to medium heat. Cover and cook for 15–20 minutes.

Purée 1/4 of the soup in a food processor or blender and return to the pot. Stir well.

Garnish with chervil and crème fraîche.

Soupe au Pistou (Pesto Soup)

The perfect summer soup.

YASSER QAHAWISH

¹/₂ cup / 120 mL	dried white beans
¹/₂ cup / 120 mL	elbow macaroni
1	whole leek, cut in half and washed
1	small onion, peeled and diced
1	carrot, peeled and diced
1	large potato, peeled and diced
4¹/₄ cups / 1 L	cold water
	salt and freshly ground black pepper
1	handful green fresh beans, washed and diced
1	zucchini, diced
1 recipe	Pesto (see below)

SERVES 6

Soak white beans overnight. Drain and discard water. Cover the white beans with fresh cold water. Bring to a boil and simmer for 45 minutes until beans are whole and firm, but not hard.

Half-cook macaroni in boiling, salted water, about 4 minutes, refresh in cold water, drain.

In a large pot, combine the leek, onion, carrot and potato with cold water, white beans, and salt and pepper. Cover, bring to a boil, reduce heat and simmer for 20 minutes. Add green beans, zucchini, and macaroni and continue simmering for another 15 minutes. Test beans and macaroni to make sure they are cooked. While the soup is cooking make the pesto.

Pesto

4	cloves garlic, peeled
1	packed handful fresh basil
¹/₂ cup / 120 mL	grated Parmesan cheese
1	ripe tomato, peeled, seeded and diced
1 cup / 240 mL	fine olive oil

Mix the pesto ingredients in a mortar and pestle, starting with the garlic and finishing the emulsion with the olive oil.

Serve the soup hot and pass around the mortar of pesto for garnish.

Mussel Mouclade

YASSER QAHAWISH

The optional liaison with egg yolks and cream brings this soup to a higher level of elegance.

SERVES 6

3¹/₂ oz. / 100 g	unsalted butter
1	medium onion, finely chopped
3	cloves garlic, finely chopped
3 lbs. / 1.35 kg	fresh mussels, well rinsed and debearded (see page 27)
1 cup / 240 mL	white wine
1	leek, cut in half, sliced, washed and drained
1	medium carrot, peeled and chopped
¹/₂ tsp. / 2.5 mL	curry paste (strength according to taste)
1	good pinch saffron
1 Tbsp. / 15 mL	flour
2 cups / 475 mL	cold water
2 cups / 475 mL	chicken stock
1 cup / 240 mL	cream
	salt and freshly ground black pepper
¹/₂	bunch fresh parsley, washed and sliced

In a large pot, melt half the butter over medium-low heat. Add onion and garlic and cover, sweating until soft and translucent.

Add mussels and white wine. Cover and turn heat to high, shaking the pot every minute or so to mix ingredients.

Cook just until all mussels have opened. Drain mussels into a strainer, reserving liquid in a measuring cup or bowl.

In the same pot over medium-low heat, melt remaining butter. Add leek and carrot, cook for a few minutes. Add curry paste, saffron and flour and cook for another few minutes, stirring.

Gradually add cold water, chicken stock and reserved mussel liquid. Bring to a boil, season with salt and pepper and simmer, uncovered, for 15 minutes.

Meanwhile, pull mussel meat from the shells and chop finely (shells can be discarded). Reduce heat to minimum, add chopped mussels to the soup with cream and parsley. Cover and simmer—without boiling—to infuse the flavours and heat through the soup.

Adjust seasoning and serve hot.

Optional
For a richer flavour, whisk 4 egg yolks with $\frac{1}{8}$ cup (80 mL) 35% cream and stir into soup. Cook slowly, stirring constantly until thickened slightly and serve at once.

For a lighter soup, blend half the mussels with 1 cup (240 mL) of the soup until smooth. Return mixture to the soup.

Cabbage Soup

YASSER QAHAWISH

A real winter soup. Complements duck confit beautifully.

1	small cabbage, washed and cut into quarters, core removed
$^1/_2$ cup / 120 mL	basmati rice, washed and drained
$3^1/_2$ oz. / 100 g	unsalted butter
1	large onion, peeled and chopped
$4^1/_4$ cups / 1 L	chicken stock
	salt and freshly ground black pepper

SERVES 6

Bring a large pot of water to a boil, add cabbage and rice, cook for 20 minutes over medium heat and drain liquid away. Reserve cabbage and rice.

Melt butter in same pot and sweat onion until translucent. Return cabbage and rice to pot, adding chicken stock, and salt and pepper. Cook for 15 minutes. Working in small batches blend to a smooth purée. Adjust seasoning.

If you like, you can garnish the soup with some oven-crisped duck confit on toast.

White Mushroom Soup

A very simple recipe to enhance pure mushroom taste. Best in the spring for the freshest, most pungent flavour.

YASSER QAHAWISH

2 lbs. / 900 g	fresh white mushrooms, quickly rinsed or brushed
3^1/$_2$ oz. / 100 g	unsalted butter
1	large onion, peeled and finely chopped
1 Tbsp. / 15 mL	all-purpose flour
1	sprig fresh thyme, leaves removed
4^1/$_4$ cups / 1 L	cold chicken stock or water (for vegetarian soup)
	salt and freshly ground black pepper
	35% cream, whipped, for garnish

SERVES 6

Grate mushrooms with food processor attachment (or by hand).

Melt butter in soup pot, add onion, cover the pot and cook slowly over medium-low heat until onion is translucent.

Add flour and cook for 3 minutes, stirring. Stir in grated mushrooms, thyme, cold chicken stock or water, and salt and pepper.

Bring to a boil and cook, covered, for 15–20 minutes over medium heat. Adjust seasoning.

For a potage consistency, purée soup in a food processor or blender. For a more rustic soup, only purée half and mix with remainder in pot.

Garnish with whipped cream.

Jerusalem Artichoke Purée with Parsnip Chips

DEBORAH REID

SERVES 6

Jerusalem Artichoke Purée

¹/₂ cup / 120 mL	unsalted butter, chilled and cubed
	salt and freshly ground black pepper
1 cup / 240 mL	sliced onion
3 lbs. / 1.35 kg	Jerusalem artichokes, washed and peeled
1¹/₂ qts. / 1.5 L	chicken stock

In a large saucepan over medium-high heat, melt ¹/₄ cup (60 mL) of the butter. When hot, add the onion and season. Reduce the heat to low and cover the pan. Add the artichokes and chicken stock and season. Bring the soup to a simmer and cook until the artichokes are very tender, about 45 minutes.

Remove the soup from the heat and purée in a blender. The finished soup should have a slightly thickened consistency—do not add too much liquid initially or the soup will be too thin; adjust to the desired consistency with the stock. With blender on high speed, emulsify the soup by adding small bits of the remaining butter. Finishing the artichoke purée with butter will give the soup a smooth, creamy texture and add gloss. Taste the soup for seasoning and strain through a fine mesh strainer. This soup can be made several days in advance and reheated.

Parsnip Chips

1 qt. / 1 L	vegetable oil
1 lb. / 455 g	parsnips, peeled and trimmed
¼ cup / 60 mL	all-purpose flour
	salt
	chives, finely chopped

Heat the vegetable oil in a suitable pot to 350°F (175°C) for deep-frying.

Using a mandoline or a sharp chef's knife, slice the parsnips lengthwise into very thin strips and place in a bowl. Just before deep-frying, toss the parsnip chips with the flour. Fry the parsnip strips in batches so as not to overcrowd the oil. The finished chip will be crisp and golden. Drain on a paper towel-lined tray and season with salt.

Gently heat the soup through over medium heat. When hot, ladle the soup into warm bowls. Just before serving, garnish with a few parsnip chips and a sprinkling of finely chopped chives. Do not garnish the purée too far in advance or the parsnip chips will go soggy. Alternately, the parsnip chips can be served in small dishes on the side.

Grilled Eggplant and Red Pepper Soup with Scallion Cream

DEBORAH REID

SERVES 6

3	red peppers
2	jalapeño peppers
4 Tbsp. / 60 mL	olive oil
1	1-lb. (455-g) eggplant
1 cup / 240 mL	red onion, thinly sliced
2	cloves garlic, peeled
6	small ripe tomatoes, coarsely chopped
1 qt. / 1 L	chicken stock
	salt and freshly ground black pepper

Scallion Cream

1	bunch scallions
2 Tbsp. / 30 mL	sherry vinegar
1/2 cup / 120 mL	sour cream
	salt and freshly ground black pepper

To prepare the peppers and eggplant, heat a grill or barbecue until very hot. Rub the red peppers and jalapeño peppers with some olive oil and place them on the grill or barbecue. Cook on one side until the skin appears charred and blistered and then turn to cook the rest of the peppers in the same manner. As the peppers are done, place them in a plastic bag or a bowl covered with plastic wrap to steam for 15 minutes. Remove the peppers from the bag or uncover the bowl and let the peppers cool. Peel off the blackened skin and remove the stems and seeds. Save the juice from steaming the peppers and reserve with the cleaned peppers. Set aside until needed.

Cut the eggplant in half lengthwise and coat with olive oil. Grill, turning as necessary, until the skin is black and the eggplant is soft. Remove from the grill and let cool. Peel away the blackened outer skin and discard. Set the flesh aside until needed. The peppers and eggplant can be prepared ahead to this point.

Heat the remaining olive oil in a large saucepan over medium heat until hot. Add the onion and cook, stirring often until lightly browned, about 5 minutes. Lower the heat, add the garlic, and cook for another 2–3 minutes, stirring frequently. Add the grilled eggplant, roasted peppers, tomatoes and chicken stock. Season with salt and pepper and bring the soup to a very gentle simmer. Cover the saucepan and cook the soup for about 35 minutes. Remove from heat and purée the soup in a blender. Strain through a fine mesh strainer into a clean saucepan and set aside until needed. This soup can be made several days in advance and reheated.

To make the scallion cream, wash and trim the green bottoms off the scallions. Set aside. Thinly slice the white part, measure out a 1/4 cup (60 mL), and set aside. Place the green tops with the sherry vinegar in a blender and purée. Strain the purée through a fine mesh strainer, pressing down on the pulp in order to extract all of the scallion juice. Discard the pulp and whisk the juice into the sour cream. Fold in the thinly sliced whites and season to taste. Refrigerate until ready to serve. This scallion cream needs to be made just prior to serving so that the onion flavour does not become too overpowering.

Gently heat the soup through over medium heat. Ladle the soup into warm soup bowls. Put the scallion cream in a small dish on the side and let each person add as much as desired to their soup.

Cream of Carrot Soup

DEBORAH REID

³/₄ cup / 180 mL unsalted butter, cubed and chilled
½ cup / 120 mL onion, sliced
4 cups / 950 mL carrots, sliced
1 sprig fresh thyme
2 qts. / 2 L chicken stock
salt and freshly ground black pepper

For the garnish
¼ cup / 60 mL unsalted butter
½ loaf unsliced white bread, crusts removed,
cut into 1-inch (2.5-cm) cubes
chives, finely chopped

SERVES 12

Melt a ¼ cup (60 mL) of the butter in a large saucepan over medium-high heat. When hot, add the onion, cover, and sweat over low heat until the onion is soft but not brown. Add the carrots and the sprig of thyme and cook for a few minutes, stirring to coat the carrots in butter. Add the chicken stock, salt and pepper, and bring the soup to a gentle simmer. Cook over medium heat until the carrots are very tender, about 45 minutes.

Remove the soup from the heat and purée in a blender. The finished soup should have a slightly thickened consistency—do not add too much liquid initially or the soup will be too thin; adjust to the desired consistency with the stock. With the blender on high speed, emulsify the soup by adding small bits of the cold cubed butter. Finishing the carrot soup with butter will give a smooth, creamy texture and add gloss. Taste the soup for seasoning and strain through a fine mesh strainer. This soup can be made several days in advance and reheated.

To garnish

Preheat the broiler in the oven.

Melt the butter over medium-high heat in a heavy cast-iron pan. Add the cubed bread and toss with the melted butter. Place the pan under the broiler and brown. Check the croutons frequently to ensure that they do not burn. When brown on one side, toss the croutons in the pan and continue to brown until they are crisp and golden all over. Drain on paper towels.

Ladle the soup into warm shallow soup bowls. Just before serving, garnish with a sprinkling of croutons and chopped chives.

Soupe au Pistou

DEBORAH REID

SERVES 12

¼ cup / 60 mL	olive oil
½ cup / 120 mL	onion, finely chopped
1	leek, white part only, thinly sliced
½ cup / 120 mL	carrots, finely chopped
½ cup / 120 mL	white turnips, finely chopped
2	stalks celery, finely chopped
	salt and freshly ground black pepper
1	sprig Italian parsley
1	sprig fresh thyme
1½ qts. / 1.5 L	chicken stock
½ cup / 120 mL	potato, finely chopped
½ cup / 120 mL	fresh green beans, finely chopped
½ cup / 120 mL	zucchini, finely chopped
½ cup / 120 mL	butternut squash, finely chopped
1 cup / 240 mL	cooked white beans
1 cup / 240 mL	small pasta, half cooked, drained and rinsed in cold water

For the pistou

2	cloves garlic, peeled and finely chopped
1	bunch fresh basil, cleaned
⅔ cup / 160 mL	extra-virgin olive oil
¾ cup / 180 mL	finely grated Parmesan cheese

Heat the ¼ cup (60 mL) olive oil in a large saucepan over medium-high heat. When hot, add the onion and leek and cook until soft but not brown. Add the carrot, turnip, celery, and salt and pepper. Cook, stirring frequently, for 5 minutes. Tie the sprigs of parsley and thyme together. Add the chicken stock, parsley and thyme sprigs, and bring to a simmer. Gently simmer for 20 minutes. Add the potatoes, green beans, zucchini and butternut squash and continue to simmer until the vegetables are tender, 15–20 minutes. Add the white beans and taste the seasoning. This soup can be made several days in advance to this point and reheated when required.

To make the pistou, place garlic and basil in the jar of a blender and process, adding the $^2/_3$ cup (160 mL) olive oil in a steady stream. Process quickly as the heat from blending will cause the pistou to lose its intense green colour and freshness. Combine the pistou and grated Parmesan in a bowl. The pistou can be made in advance and refrigerated until needed.

In a saucepan, combine the soup base and the pasta. Do not add the pasta too far in advance of serving the soup as it will expand in the liquid and become overcooked. Gently heat the soup through over medium heat, checking the seasoning. Just before serving, stir in the pistou and let the soup heat through for 3 minutes to allow the garlic to lose some of its pungent edge. Ladle the soup into warm soup bowls and serve.

Asparagus Soup

DEBORAH REID

2 lbs. / 900 g green asparagus
3 Tbsp. / 45 mL unsalted butter
1 onion, finely chopped
 salt and freshly ground black pepper
1^1/$_2$ qts. / 1.5 L chicken stock
^{1}/$_4$ cup / 60 mL unsalted butter, cubed and chilled
 sour cream, for garnish
 finely chopped chives, for garnish

SERVES 12

Clean the asparagus by breaking off and discarding the tough fibrous ends. Working with 4 to 6 spears at a time, line the asparagus up so that all the tips are even. Cut the tips into 1^1/$_2$-inch (3.8-cm) lengths. Set aside and cut the remaining stalks into ^{1}/$_2$-inch (1.2-cm) pieces.

In a saucepan, melt the butter over medium-high heat. When hot, add the onion and salt and pepper. Sauté the onion, stirring frequently, for 5 minutes until soft but not brown. Add half the chopped asparagus stalks to the onion mixture and sauté for another 2–3 minutes. Add the chicken stock, season and simmer the soup for about 20 minutes or until the asparagus is tender.

Bring a large pot of salted water to the boil. Have ready a stainless steel bowl with cold water and ice. Blanch the reserved asparagus tips in the boiling water until just tender. Immediately plunge them into the cold water. This process is known as refreshing and will immediately stop the cooking process, preserving the vibrant green colour of the asparagus. When cool, remove the asparagus tips and drain, setting aside until needed. Blanch the remaining chopped asparagus stalks in the same manner and when cool, drain and set aside until needed.

Remove the soup from the heat and fill the blender jar halfway with the hot soup. Add a handful of the blanched asparagus stalks, season, and process the soup until smooth. Remove the lid of the blender jar while it is running and add a few small bits of the chilled unsalted butter to the soup while it is processing. Continue blending the soup after the addition of butter to ensure that it has been completely emulsified. Strain the soup into a stainless steel bowl which is sitting in an ice bath. Process the remaining soup in the same manner. This soup can be made several days in advance and reheated or served cold.

The reserved asparagus tips can be added to the soup as it is being reheated. Do not boil the soup and do not let it heat for an excessively long time as this will destroy the vibrant green colour. When hot, ladle the soup into warm bowls and garnish with a dollop of sour cream and finely chopped chives.

The Best Winter Soup for Myself

MICHAEL STADTLÄNDER

Kill a chicken and clean it. Put it in a pot with bay leaves, thyme, salt and pepper, a little nutmeg, cut-up carrots, sliced leek and chopped celery root. Cover with cold water, bring to a boil, then cook at a simmer until the chicken meat is tender. When the chicken is cooked, remove the meat and return it to the broth. Remove any fat that's floating on top of the broth.

In another pot, boil some Japanese rice. When it's cooked, put it in a bowl and ladle soup overtop. Sprinkle with chopped parsley and serve.

Bingo.

SERVES 4

Cold Summer Fruit Soup with Vanilla Anglaise

MICHAEL STADTLÄNDER

1	vanilla bean
1 cup / 240 mL	milk
1 cup / 240 mL	35% cream
3½ oz. / 100 g	vanilla sugar
5	large egg yolks
1 cup / 240 mL	strawberries
1 cup / 240 mL	raspberries
1 cup / 240 mL	blackcurrants
1 cup / 240 mL	rhubarb, cut into 1-inch (2.5-cm) lengths
2 cups / 475 mL	apple cider
1	bottle Riesling wine
	berry sugar to taste
	sprigs of fresh mint to garnish

SERVES 4

Cut the vanilla bean open lengthwise and scrape out the seeds. Put the scraped bean into a pot with the milk, cream and half the vanilla sugar. Bring the mixture to a boil.

In a bowl set over boiling water, whip the egg yolks with the remaining vanilla sugar until the mixture is creamy. Add the vanilla cream to the egg mixture just as the vanilla cream begins to boil. Stir until the cream is completely incorporated. Refrigerate until cool.

Strain out the vanilla bean. Combine half the strawberries, raspberries, blackcurrants and rhubarb with the cider and the wine in a large saucepan and cook until the fruit has softened. Purée in a blender and strain through a fine sieve. Return the fruit to the heat and bring it to a boil. When the puréed fruit is boiling, add the remaining fruit. Just before the fruit mixture boils again, remove it from the heat and add berry sugar to taste (not too much as it should be refreshing). Keep the fruit soup cool in the refrigerator.

To serve, ladle some soup into chilled bowls, top with vanilla anglaise and garnish with sprigs of fresh mint.

Potato-Quark Purée with Lentils and Roast Suckling Pig Chop

MICHAEL STADTLÄNDER

Dry rub for the pork

	pork fat
	caraway seeds
1	bay leaf
	cloves
	thyme
	marjoram
	parsley
	rosemary
	lovage
	salt and fresh ground black pepper

SERVES 6

For the soup

6	suckling pig chops in one piece
1 Tbsp. / 15 mL	rendered duck fat
1 lb. / 455 g	potatoes, preferably German Butter Ball
3/4 cup / 180 mL	35% cream
1 cup / 180 mL	unsalted butter
	salt
	fresh nutmeg
2	onions
2	cloves garlic
1/4 cup / 60 mL	lentils, soaked overnight
4 1/4 cups / 1 L	chicken stock
1	bay leaf
2	sprigs fresh thyme
1 tsp. / 5 mL	balsamic vinegar
2 Tbsp. / 30 mL	mustard
	salt and freshly ground black pepper
	maple syrup
3 1/2 oz. / 100 g	Quark

Rub pork fat and herbs all over the suckling pig chops, season with salt and pepper, and refrigerate overnight. The proportion of herbs is entirely up to you. You don't need to use every one that is listed in the ingredients.

Render the duck fat. Take fat from duck trimmings, chop and heat in a cool oven until fat runs out. Strain fat and reserve.

Boil the potatoes in their skins until tender. When they are cooked, peel them and put them through a potato ricer. Heat the cream and add it to the potatoes with the butter, salt and a few gratings of nutmeg. Mash well and keep warm.

While the potatoes are cooking, chop the onions and garlic. Warm the duck fat in a large soup pot and add the onion and garlic. Cook slowly, stirring occasionally, until the onion and garlic have caramelized. Add the lentils and cover with chicken stock. Add the bay leaf and thyme sprigs. Boil until the lentils have softened. Remove the bay leaf and thyme, then add the vinegar, mustard, salt and pepper, and a little maple syrup.

To prepare the pork, heat more pork fat in a skillet and sear the meaty side of the pork. Flip it to the skin side and roast in a 450°F (230°C) oven until the crackling is crispy. The chops should still be moist and juicy. Let the meat rest for 10 minutes.

Meanwhile, finish the soup. Heat the potato purée and lentils in separate pots. At the very last moment, add Quark to the potato purée. Put a little bit of each mixture in each bowl. Cut up one chop per serving and place the pieces on top of the soup.

MICHAEL STADTLÄNDER

Cold Yogurt-Buttermilk Lemon Soup with Grated Pumpernickel

2¼ cups / 535 mL	full-fat yogurt
2¼ cups / 535 mL	buttermilk
3	organic lemons, zest and juice of
5	slices pumpernickel

Stir the yogurt to make it liquid. Add the buttermilk, juice and zest from the lemons, and refrigerate until well chilled.

Grate the pumpernickel in a food processor until it resembles medium-coarse crumbs.

Serve the soup in cold bowls, with pumpernickel sprinkled over top.

SERVES 4

Soup with Cabbage, Roasted Red Beets and Barbecued Pickerel

MICHAEL STADTLÄNDER

1 Tbsp. / 15 mL	duck fat
1–2	small onions, sliced
1/4	head white cabbage
3/4 cup / 180 mL	Riesling wine
4 1/4 cups / 1 L	chicken stock
	marjoram*
	winter savoury*
	thyme*
	caraway*
	chives*
	sea salt and freshly ground black pepper
6	red beets
1 cup / 240 mL	apple cider
1 Tbsp. / 15 mL	apple cider vinegar
1 tsp. / 5 mL	olive oil
1	pickerel fillet, about 5 oz. (150 g)

SERVES 6

*In any combination or proportion you prefer.

Heat duck fat and add the onions. Sweat the onions until transparent and add the cabbage. Braise until cabbage has wilted then add the wine, chicken stock, chopped marjoram, winter savoury and thyme. Cook until the cabbage is tender, but not mushy. Season with salt and pepper.

Set aside half the beets. Peel and juice the remaining beets in a food processor. Strain and reserve the juice. In a saucepan, heat the beet juice with the apple cider and apple cider vinegar, and reduce to a glaze consistency. Strain and add the vinegar. Meanwhile, roast the remaining beets, peeled and cut into whatever shape you like, in the olive oil in a 400°F (200°C) oven until cooked but still crunchy. Add the beet glaze.

Season the pickerel with salt and pepper and barbecue over maple wood embers until medium-cooked.

Heat the cabbage soup and ladle it into bowls with the beets and the beet glaze. Swirl the soups around, but don't mix them together. Slice the pickerel and place the slices on top of the soup. Serve.

Cream of Lobster Soup

MASAYUKI TAMARU

SERVES 4

1	1½-lb. (680-g) lobster
2 Tbsp. / 30 mL	olive oil
1	clove garlic
⅓ cup / 80 mL	onion, diced
⅓ cup / 80 mL	carrot, diced
⅓ cup / 80 mL	fennel, diced
⅓ cup / 80 mL	leek, diced
⅓ cup / 80 mL	celery, diced
¼ cup / 60 mL	cognac
2	tomatoes, seeded and chopped
3	sprigs parsley, leaves only
¼ cup / 60 mL	white wine
½ cup / 120 mL	chicken stock
½ cup / 120 mL	fish stock
2¼ cups / 535 mL	35% cream
1 Tbsp. / 15 mL	unsalted butter
	salt and freshly ground black pepper
3 Tbsp. / 45 mL	fresh chervil, chopped
1 tsp. / 5 mL	cognac

Cook the lobster in boiling water for 5 minutes. Remove and plunge into ice water to cool.

Remove meat from lobster shell. Break shell into small pieces.

Heat olive oil and sauté garlic until fragrant. Add shell pieces and sauté. Add onion, carrot, fennel, leek and celery. Sauté for 4 minutes. Add cognac and flambé. Add tomatoes and parsley and reduce. Add white wine and reduce until almost all the liquid has evaporated. Add chicken and fish stocks and simmer for 10 minutes. Stir in cream and simmer for another 10 minutes. Strain through a fine sieve. Swirl butter through soup and add salt and pepper to taste. Sprinkle chervil over the soup and drizzle in 1 tsp. (5 mL) of cognac.

Place lobster meat in the bowls and pour soup over top. Serve.

Chilled Avocado Soup with Stuffed Tomato

MASAYUKI TAMARU

5	small tomatoes
30	green peas
2	avocados
10	small shrimp
2	scallops, diced
1/2	lemon, juice of
2 Tbsp. / 30 mL	mayonnaise
1 cup + 3 Tbsp / 285 mL	35% cream
1/2	onion
1 Tbsp. / 15 mL	unsalted butter
2 cups / 475 mL	chicken consommé (see page 123)
1 cup / 240 mL	milk
	salt
	cayenne pepper
pinch	fresh tarragon, chopped

SERVES 5

Blanch tomatoes in boiling water. Peel, cut off bottom, seed and hollow out each tomato. Salt tomato cavity and put all the tomatoes upside down to drain.

Blanch green peas in salted boiling water. Take one avocado and dice half, cut the other half into cubes.

Blanch shrimp in salted, boiling water with half the lemon juice for 2 minutes. Plunge into ice water. Peel and devein, cut into cubes.

Mix peas, avocado, scallops and shrimp with mayonnaise, 3 Tbsp. (45 mL) cream and remaining lemon juice. Fill tomatoes. Keep refrigerated.

In a soup pot, sauté onion in butter. Add consommé and cook for 20 minutes. Cool. Pour the mixture into a blender. Add the second avocado and purée well. Strain into a stainless steel bowl. Mix in milk, remaining 1 cup (240 mL) cream, salt, cayenne and tarragon.

Ladle soup into soup bowls. Garnish each bowl with a stuffed tomato.

White Asparagus Soup

MASAYUKI TAMARU

2 Tbsp. / 30 mL	unsalted butter
1	onion, sliced
1 lb. / 455 g	white asparagus, sliced
4^1/$_4$ cups / 1 L	water
1 cup / 240 mL	milk
1	5-inch (12.5-cm) baguette, crust removed
1 cup / 240 mL	35% cream
	salt and freshly ground black pepper
1 recipe	Corn Cream (see below)

SERVES 5

Melt butter in a soup pot. Gently sauté onion until soft and translucent, about 5 minutes. Add asparagus and sauté for 3 minutes. Add water, milk and baguette, and bring to a boil. Simmer for 10 minutes. Remove from heat and process in a blender or food processor. Strain through a fine sieve. Return mixture to soup pot, add cream and bring to a boil. Season to taste. Serve with corn cream drizzled on top.

Corn Cream

1	cob fresh corn
2 cups / 475 mL	water
^{1}/$_2$ cup / 120 mL	35% cream
	salt

Remove kernels from cob. Boil cob in water for 10 minutes. Remove cob from liquid, add kernels, and cook for 5 minutes. Add cream and salt. Purée in a blender. Strain, reserving the "cream."

Pheasant and Lentil Soup with Quenelles

MASAYUKI TAMARU

1	pheasant
2 Tbsp. / 30 mL	unsalted butter
1^1/$_2$	onions, sliced
^{1}/$_2$ cup / 120 mL	madeira wine
6 cups / 1.5 L	chicken stock
3^1/$_2$ oz. / 100 g	lentils
^{1}/$_2$ cup / 120 mL	carrot, diced
^{1}/$_2$ cup / 120 mL	onion, diced
^{1}/$_2$ cup / 120 mL	celery, diced
^{1}/$_2$ cup / 120 mL	bacon pieces, chopped
10 oz. / 300 mL	35% cream
	salt and freshly ground black pepper
	nutmeg, freshly grated
^{1}/$_2$	egg white

SERVES 5

Bone breast of pheasant and set aside. Cut the rest of the pheasant bones into pieces. Sauté pheasant pieces with butter. When meat is brown, add onion and sauté well. Add madeira wine, flambé and reduce. Add chicken stock and simmer for 2 hours. Strain with a fine sieve.

Place lentils, carrot, onion, celery and bacon in a soup pot. Cover with cold water and cook until soft. When cooked, reserve 5 Tbsp. (75 mL) of lentil and vegetable mixture to garnish each bowl.

Purée the rest of the lentil mixture with ^{3}/$_4$ of the pheasant stock. (Keep remaining stock to cook pheasant quenelles.) Add half the cream. Season. Add butter. This can be made ahead and reheated when needed.

To make the pheasant quenelles, put 3^1/$_2$ oz. (100 g) of breast through a food processor. Add salt and pepper, nutmeg and egg white. Combine in food processor. Add the remaining cream and combine in food processor.

Bring remaining pheasant stock to the boil. Lower heat. Drop teaspoonfuls of puréed pheasant into the simmering stock. Cook for 3 minutes. Remove carefully with slotted spoon.

Slice remaining pheasant breast, season and sauté with butter.

Ladle soup into bowls. Garnish with vegetable mixture, quenelles and breast of pheasant.

Dashi

HIRO YOSHIDA

Dashi is a combination of kelp seaweed and bonito flakes. Each of the following recipes contains dashi.

Bring 4$^1/_4$ cups (1 L) of cold water containing 3 inches (7.5 cm) of kelp to the boil. Just before the water boils remove the seaweed, turn off the heat and add 3$^1/_2$ oz. (100 mL) of cold water and 1 handful (20 g) of bonito flakes. Let the infusion settle for a few minutes and strain.

Miso (Soybean) Soup

4$^1/_4$ cups / 1 L	dashi (see above)
1$^3/_4$ oz. / 50 g	miso paste
2 cups / 475 mL	seasonal vegetables, chopped (eggplant, carrot, turnip, or whatever you prefer)

SERVES 4

Heat the dashi and the miso. Chop the vegetables into bite-size pieces, add them to the dashi broth and cook until tender, but not mushy.

Serve hot.

Chawan Mushi (Steamed Egg Custard)

HIRO YOSHIDA

2 cups / 475 mL	dashi (see page 112)
2	eggs, beaten
$1/4$ tsp. / 1.2 mL	salt
1 tsp. / 5 mL	light soy sauce
$1/4$ tsp. / 1.2 mL	mirin
$1/2$ tsp. / 2.5 mL	sake
4	pieces yozu zest (Japanese tangerine)
1 cup / 240 mL	combination of shrimp, chicken, ginko nuts, bamboo shoots

Combine all ingredients and steam, covered, in a small saucepan for 10–12 minutes. Serve immediately.

SERVES 4

Dobin Mushi
(Steamed Pinetree Mushroom Soup)

2 cups / 475 mL	dashi (see page 112)
$1/4$ tsp. / 1.2 mL	mirin
1 tsp. / 5 mL	sake
$1/4$ tsp. / 1.2 mL	salt
$1 1/2$ tsp. / 7.5 mL	light soy sauce
12	pinetree mushrooms, sliced
4	wedges sudachi (Japanese lime)

SERVES 4

Combine all ingredients and steam, covered, in a small saucepan for 7–8 minutes.

Surinagashi (Cold Green Pea Potage)

HIRO YOSHIDA

2	cloves garlic, roasted
	olive oil
	salt and freshly ground pepper
2 lbs. / 900 g	fresh peas, shelled
1 tsp. / 5 mL	salt
6 oz. / 170 mL	dashi (see page 112) [+4^1/$_2$ cups / +1L]
1	medium onion, sautéed
	handful of spinach, sautéed
dash	light soy sauce

SERVES 4

To roast garlic, cut the top off the heads to expose most of the cloves; remove excess paper from heads. Fold aluminum foil round garlic, drizzle each head with olive oil and season well. Cover with foil and roast in a 400°F (200°C) oven for 40 minutes, until the garlic has softened. Let cool enough to squeeze each clove out of its paper skin.

Boil fresh green peas with a pinch of salt. Strain and blend peas to a smooth paste in a blender with 6 oz. (170 mL) dashi, sautéed onions, roasted garlic and boiled spinach. Mix 7 oz. (200 mL) of the green pea purée with 4^1/$_4$ cups (1 L) of dashi, ^{1}/$_4$ tsp. (1.2 mL) salt and ^{1}/$_4$ tsp. (1.2 mL) light soy sauce.

the chefs
stocks & pots
index

SUZANNE BABY
THE GALLERY GRILL AT HART HOUSE

Suzanne Baby is a native Torontonian who began her career as an apprentice in the kitchen at The Windsor Arms hotel. She then held positions at Splendido and Lakes before becoming Executive Chef at The Gallery Grill at the University of Toronto's Hart House.

LAUREN BOYINGTON
LAW SOCIETY OF UPPER CANADA

Much of Lauren Boyington's career has been at restaurants run by Jamie Kennedy. She began as an apprentice at Palmerston, followed by a stint at The Founder's Club, then returned to Palmerston as sous-chef with Kennedy. She worked with Gary Hoyer at Millie's in Toronto before assuming her current position with Yasser Qahawish at the Law Society.

KEITH FROGGETT
SCARAMOUCHE

Keith Froggett hails from England, but he has been one of Toronto's pre-eminent chefs since the early 1980s when he worked at Fenton's. Since 1986, he has been Executive Chef at Scaramouche, where he has been responsible for turning out some of Toronto's most consistently excellent and creative cuisine.

BETSY GUTNIK
UNIVERSITY COLLEGE

Having made the professional transition from architect to chef, Betsy Gutnik completed the Italian program at George Brown College and went on to study in Italy. Her first restaurant position was at Biaggio Ristorante in the St. Lawrence Hall. After Biaggio, Betsy worked in Jamie Kennedy's commissary kitchen for JK ROM before accepting the position of Executive Chef in charge of food services at University College.

LINDA HAYNES
ACE BAKERY

Linda Haynes is co-founder and co-owner of ACE Bakery Limited, a specialty gourmet bakery providing freshly-baked artisanal breads in Ontario. Ten percent of ACE's profits is donated to Calmeadow, a non-profit organization Linda co-founded with her husband Martin Cornell in 1983. Calmeadow helps people, primarily in the developing world, to gain access to credit and become economically self-reliant.

GARY HOYER
MILLIE'S GOURMET WAREHOUSE AND BISTRO

Gary Hoyer is originally from Pittsburgh, PA. He made his way to Toronto in the mid-1970s to work as a saucier at the Three Small Rooms. Gary went on to become Executive Chef at The Trolley, then at The Windsor Arms. Currently, he is Chef/Owner of Millie's, a favourite brunch and shopping spot in North Toronto.

SIMON KATTAR
A LA CARTE KITCHEN

In addition to his all-important function as Executive Chef at The Gardiner Museum's A La Carte restaurant, Simon

Kattar runs one of Toronto's best-known catering operations: A La Carte Kitchen. With a host of upmarket clients, including Tiffany, Simon has his hands full. In addition to his busy professional life, he donates hours of his time to the children's charity he founded, Waladi.

JAMIE KENNEDY
JK ROM

Jamie Kennedy apprenticed at The Windsor Arms Hotel before spending three years as a journeyman cook in Europe. He returned to Toronto, to the position of co-chef at Scaramouche with Michael Stadtlaender from 1980 to 1983. Through the mid-1980s and early 1990s, Jamie was Chef and partner at Palmerston Restaurant. In 1994, he opened JK ROM at Toronto's Royal Ontario Museum, where he is Executive Chef/Owner.

MARTIN KOUPRIE
PANGAEA

Martin Kouprie established himself as one of Toronto's brightest culinary stars with his work at Pronto Ristorante and at Jump before he went on to open Pangaea to great acclaim. Known for his modern, sophisticated approach to seasonal highlights, Martin is one of the city's most consistently excellent chefs.

SUSUR LEE
SUSUR

Often named as one of the world's top chefs, Susur Lee emigrated from Hong Kong to Canada in the early 1980s. He worked at Peter Pan on Toronto's Queen St. West before opening Lotus in 1986. A decade of success at Lotus was followed by career development in Singapore and New York before he returned to Toronto to open Susur in the Fall of 2000.

CHRISTOPHER MCDONALD
AVALON

Chris McDonald perfected his craft in fine restaurants all over the world, including Chez Panisse in San Francisco. He has opened some of Toronto's most successful restaurants, including Santa Fe Bar and Grill and Centro. Avalon is one of Toronto's most frequently top-rated dining experiences.

MARGARET MACKAY
Bb33

Margaret Mackay began her career as an apprentice at Toronto's Sheraton Hotel. She then worked with Chris Klugman at Oro before settling in for four years as Executive Sous-Chef at JK ROM with Jamie Kennedy. Since the summer of 2000, Margaret has been Executive Chef at Bb33 in the Metropolitan Hotel.

KENNETH PEACE
HUMMINGBIRD CENTRE

Ken Peace has been known for years as one of the most creative forces in Toronto's Hummingbird Centre. As Executive Chef there, he consistently turns out lavish and spectacular dinners on a challenging pre-curtain schedule. Ken is also well known for exquisite special-events catering.

YASSER QAHAWISH
LAW SOCIETY OF UPPER CANADA

Yasser Qahawish studied cookery at George Brown College in Toronto before working his way through France and Spain at several Michelin three-star restaurants. His impeccable European training is apparent in the food that is presented by Chef Qahawish and his team at the Law Society.

DEBORAH REID
STRATFORD CHEFS SCHOOL

Deborah Reid has been a cookery instructor at the Stratfod Chefs School since 1994. She has worked at both The Old Prune and Rundles in Stratford. Her culinary career has been enriched through her studies in Italy, France, the US, and at London's River Café.

MICHAEL STADTLÄNDER
EIGENSINN FARM

Recently named as one of the top ten restaurants in the world, Eigensinn is the home and brainchild of Michael and Nobuyo Stadtländer. Michael trained in Germany and Switzerland, where he met Jamie Kennedy. The two cooked at Scaramouche together from 1980 to 1983, when Michael left to open Stadtländer's. Eigensinn Farm has been in operation since 1992.

MASAYUKI TAMARU
CRUSH

Masayuki Tamaru was part of the opening brigade in 1994 when JK ROM was launched. He left in 1998 to work as sous-chef for Didier Leroy at The Fifth, where he stayed as kitchen chef until 2000. Masayuki is now Executive Chef at the new Crush in Toronto.

HIRO YOSHIDA
HIRO SUSHI

Hiro Yoshida first came to Toronto from his native Japan in 1983. He worked at Takesushi until 1987 before moving on to Katsura and Sasaya. The early 1990s were taken up with full-time catering before Hiro Sushi opened at its original Church St. location. Now on King St., Hiro Sushi is a destination restaurant for lovers of top-quality sushi in Toronto.

Artistry created the inspired soups and bowls in this book. In pottery or cooking, the skilful use of tools and an understanding of techniques shape the finished dish. The art of soup starts with simple fundamentals that translate from the cheery warm stove at home right into the stainless glow of a busy restaurant. Truly, anyone can make a soup that's a feast for the eyes and the spirit. New cooks can hone their skills in a kitchen stocked with simple basics. When it's time to raise the bar and add a touch of refinement, some extras may be called for.

Soups come in many styles. In this book, the soups are as varied as the chefs, their culinary influences and shopping baskets. Even with this diversity, it's easy to highlight some soup-making fundamentals and techniques. Read the recipe for your inspiration. The soup is for the rest of you.

THE SOUP POT

Form follows function in the kitchen. After reading a soup recipe, it should be easy to decide what pot will suit the method, style and volume of the recipe. Purposely opposite in shape, the pots favoured for soups are Dutch ovens and stockpots. Dutch ovens tend to be twice as wide as they are high, combining the width of a skillet on the bottom with deep sides for holding liquids. A well-constructed pot with a thicker bottom and wider shape makes Dutch ovens (known as French ovens to some) perfect for recipes beginning with sautéed vegetables or browned meats, that build the soup in layers. This style of soup often enjoys a good simmer to thicken and build flavour.

Stocks are fundamental in soup making. Combine water with flavourful base ingredients—vegetarian, bird, fish, meat —and simmer to infused perfection. The taller chimney shape of the stockpots keeps evaporation of the valuable broth to a minimum before it is strained or waits for tasty additions. Stockpots are perfect pasta cooking pots as well, but not all stockpots are created equally. With water as the main ingredient, lightweight pots will perform well enough but their shape and weight may not make them as versatile. Any soup that begins with a stock or broth as a base, from miso to chicken noodle, will simmer beautifully in the tall shape. Stockpots and Dutch ovens are sized by volume in quarts or litres (so close they are considered the same). A simple rule—keeping in mind that rules can be broken—is that a household that finds a four-quart or four-litre Dutch oven useful should be happy with double volume as a stockpot, eight quarts or litres. Another simple gauge for stock-making: divide a stockpot's quarts in half (for pounds) or litres by four (for kilos) to estimate how much ingredients in weight the pot will hold before the water is added. As always, buy to suit your own needs in the kitchen and invest in the best equipment you can afford.

SEPARATING BROTH FROM BOUILLON

In busy lives stock-making can be therapeutic or just another item on the ever-expanding "to do" list. With all the choices in commercial broths, pastes and cubes available, can they help a busy soup-maker? Some classic soups are made from pastes, miso for example. Until reconstituted with water, pastes are too intense to be palatable. They can help a soup with lots of flavourful ingredients, but all that water is not going to add body. A spoonful or a cube of commercial stock base can give a little flavour boost but will come to the forefront in soups served cold, so always use your best stock for chilled soups. Of course, any soup where the broth has the leading role—chicken noodle, French onion—deserves body and rich flavour. Stock is a necessity.

There are better brands of pastes and cubes on the market. Many have no MSG and there are even vegetarian options that offer chicken and beef flavours. Specialty food stores offer some great alternative brands. Keep them in the cupboard for soup emergencies if you need a bowl as first-aid.

SWEATING AND SAUTÉING

Chefs have their own lingo. When the term "sweating" appears in a recipe, it usually means that vegetables are being cooked gently with a small amount of fat. The heat should be low and as the natural juices are released, the vegetables soften. At home, we work in smaller amounts.

Covering the pot will keep the moisture from evaporating or a spoonful of broth or water can help if the vegetables are drying. Choose a pot rather than a skillet. Sweating vegetables softens and heightens flavour without browning.

Sautéing is a quick cooking method, using fat to speed the browning process. Over medium heat, stirring to prevent scorching or sticking, the moisture evaporates quickly, promoting browning and adding a rich layer of flavour. Think of how an onion changes as it is coaxed from raw to a beautiful brown. A skillet or sauté pan is usually the pan of choice. If a soup begins with a layer of sautéed or sweated vegetables, a Dutch oven may be the perfect candidate for one-pot cooking.

THE PERFECT TEXTURE

Velvety puréed soups or crystal clear consommé, mysteriously perfect. The secret to a perfectly puréed soup is to work in small batches. Flavour and texture will be better if the liquids and solids are separated, the solids puréed with as little of the liquid as necessary, combining them again to adjust the finished soup. Puréeing the solids separately prevents a starchy flavour and seasoning can be adjusted before adding the liquid and adjusting the texture. Blenders are excellent for smooth soups. Work in small batches. For piping hot soup, remove the cap in the centre of the lid to allow the pressure of steam to escape and cover with a clean, folded tea towel. Hold the cover firmly in place and pulse carefully.

After the first pulse the steam will have escaped and the processing will go smoothly. For a manual approach, a food mill or a chinois strainer will work. Again, separate as much of the soup solids from the liquids as possible, pass through the mill or chinois and introduce the liquids to adjust the texture. Many cooks—traditional and professional— love the food mill.

For straining broths, a strainer lined with layers of cheesecloth will take away fine particles. For vegetable broths, a paper coffee filter works as well.

Some things just do taste better the second day. Long simmered soups with layers of ingredients, like a Tuscan ribollita or potato-leek, often emerge with a more interesting flavour the second day when each ingredient becomes part of the infusion. Without the benefit of heat to pull the flavours together, chilled soups need time for the same infusion to take place, so always make them a day ahead. Broth-based soups vary. Asian broth soups are superb freshly made, with the noodles and vegetables crisp and bright. Meat and poultry broth can always be made ahead, so rather than freezing or storing the soup, add pasta and vegetables later and they'll retain their integrity. The next step is freezing and the same rules apply. Soups, stocks and broths are perfect candidates for the freezer. Once thawed, reheat to refresh the flavour.

The most commonly used stocks are veal, chicken and white fish. The neutral flavours are the most versatile. Stocks can be made from beef, lamb, pork, shellfish, etc. and their stronger definitive flavours will characterize their uses. Apart from flavour, meat- and poultry-based stocks add body. Stocks made from vegetables and fish offer flavour but won't enhance texture—just as with bouillon cubes or canned broth.

Stocks vary with cuisines. Asian stocks are milder and have a high ratio of water to keep the flavours subtle. Stocks in Italian cuisines are often laced with wine. Choose according to use.

Stocks also reflect the quality of the ingredients and the care taken. Clean trimmings, less than perky vegetables and flavourful stems of herbs work well. Bitter peelings, mouldy or strongly flavoured vegetables will taint the stock. Keep a resealable plastic bag in the freezer to gather meat and vegetable trimmings. Add them to a new batch of stock or make a small quick batch for emergencies.

Good stocks are consistent—pay attention to proportion and balance. A good rule to follow visually with any stock is to cover the bones and mirepoix by two fingers' width of water. Mirepoix is also important. Too much carrot will make the stock overly sweet. Too much green leek will take over the stock. The larger the bones, the longer the stock cooks. The mirepoix should be cut to match the cooking times and texture of the base. Mirepoix for fish stocks should be finely diced, veal stock mirepoix may be coarsely chopped. Short-cooking fish stock often begins with a brief sweating of the vegetables to encourage best flavour; brown stocks benefit from browned vegetables.

Do not cover and do not stir. The bones will settle and a foam will rise to the surface. Skimming removes the undesirable foam, which can cloud the stock or turn it bitter. Covering the pot forces the foam back into the simmering liquid, so always cook stocks uncovered.

Do not overcook or undercook stocks. As volume increases so does cooking time but overcooking produces bitter cloudy stock. Better to strain and reduce than overcook the bones. A good rule is to measure the cooking time from when the stock has been skimmed.

Well-made stocks are the backbone of cooking but don't be afraid to make quick stocks or short stocks for everyday use.

Freeze stocks in plastic containers that will release the frozen stock with a simple running under the tap to warm the container or fit in the microwave. The frozen stock will melt quickly for use. For intense stocks, such as demi-glace, freeze in small containers or ice-cube trays for quick sauce making.

CHICKEN STOCK: WHITE AND BROWN

A most basic, versatile and fundamental stock, both in ingredients and method.

Backs and necks are cheap and abundant for stock making; adding wings, feet or stewing hens adds flavour and body to the stocks. Roasting the bones for brown stock eliminates the fat, making the stock naturally leaner even before skimming. Chicken stock is versatile enough to use on other poultry, meats and even strong flavoured fish.

INGREDIENTS

5 lbs / 2.25 kg chicken parts—back, necks, wings or a stewing hen when available

1 large onion, chopped

2 carrots, peeled and chopped

2 stalks celery, chopped
bouquet garni: sprigs of thyme, parsley and bay leaf

12 peppercorns

pinch salt

cold water

FOR WHITE STOCK:

Place the bones in a large stockpot and cover with water by 2 inches (5 cm). Bring to a high simmer, turning down the heat to maintain the slow bubbling.

After 10 minutes, foam will appear. Use a ladle to skim away the foam as it appears. Skimming the foam keeps the stock from being bitter and cloudy.

Add the chopped mirepoix, bouquet garni and seasonings. Add water to maintain the 2 inch (5 cm) level. From the point the pot returns to a bubbling simmer, cook for 2 hours.

After the stock has cooked, strain the liquid into a clean pot or bowl. Discard the flavour base. Allow the fat to come to the surface and use a ladle to skim away the excess. Another method is to use a degreasing cup. This is good for small batches but not practical in commercial kitchens. For a more refined stock, free of herbs and bits of chicken, strain through triple mesh stainless strainer or layers of cheesecloth. Cool to room temperature.

Once the stock has cooled in the refrigerator, the last of the fat may be skimmed from the surface. Chicken stock keeps up to one week in the refrigerator but should be frozen for longer storage.

FOR BROWN STOCK:
Brown the chicken parts in a preheated 400°F (200°C)oven or in a heavy skillet in batches. In the oven, the parts will brown evenly; in the skillet the chicken will have colour but will not cook through.

The vegetables may be added to the roasting pan in the last half hour of cooking or browned in a skillet.

Pour off the pan fat and deglaze the pan, adding the liquid to the stockpot.

Follow the White Stock method for the remainder of the cooking process.

CONSOMMÉ
SERVES 3
6 cups / 1.5 L chicken, duck or beef stock
1/2 lb. / 250 g beef shank, ground (or lean ground beef)
1/2 cup / 120 mL onions, finely diced
1/3 cup / 80 mL carrots, finely diced
1/3 cup / 80 mL celery , finely diced
1/4 cup / 60 mL leeks, finely diced
1/2 cup / 120 mL egg white
cracked black pepper

Mix together the beef, onions, celery , carrots, black pepper, leeks and egg whites. This is the "clearmeat." Combine in a saucepan with the stock. Slowly bring to a boil, stirring only at the beginning to combine and keep the clearmeat from sticking to the bottom of the pot.

When the mixture reaches boiling point, reduce immediately to a simmer and stop stirring. With luck, a "chimney" will form in your "raft." Do not disturb the geysers. Allow to simmer uncovered for 1 hour.

Allow to rest for 15 minutes. Strain through cheesecloth without pressing the solids. It is best to ladle consommé out of the pot, rather than pouring. Degrease, adjust seasoning and garnish.

GARNISHES FOR CONSOMMÉ:
1 OR 2 TBSP. (15 OR 30 ML) PER SERVING
Julienne vegetables
Tomato concasse
Sliced bits of cooked game or meat
Fresh herbs

Vegetables should be blanched and refreshed. Garnishes should be precisely cut.

Consommés can be flavoured with fortified wines such as Madeira or Port. Use sparingly—1 Tbsp. (15 mL) per serving.

Glenys Morgan